Fifteen Inspiring Christian Biographies

It's My Turn

compiled by Kingdom Building Ministries

how you
can be
mentored by
Christianity's
greatest leaders

foreword by John C. Maxwell

Contents

Foreword

by John C. Maxwell

I have always been a student of history. As long as I can remember, I have been intrigued and improved by reading the accounts of great men and women who, by their commitment and passion, have changed the course of human history.

Somewhere along the way, however, in our market driven culture, we've embraced the notion that something has to be "new" to be good, or relevant, or meaningful. That just isn't true. Some of the most profound truths were discovered and recorded by people such as Amy Carmichael, J. Hudson Taylor, Keith Green and others. What's more, I believe our generation must *rediscover* those truths—today.

In this volume, you will have your chance to do just that. In a way, this book represents your opportunity to be "mentored" by some of Christianity's greatest leaders. Laid out in a very "user friendly" fashion, are some of the stories, thoughts, and contributions of world changers throughout history. Included are opportunities for you to interact with the lessons you learn. I encourage you to absorb these pages. Prayerfully consider why God was able to use their lives in such significant ways-and what He wants to say to you through their stories. This is the kind of devotional guide I'd like my own kids to be reading.

Each of these great leaders are gone, now. Their mentoring services live on, however, through the words of books like this one. I commend it to you. May you be inspired to action as you read and then respond as a good apprentice would—saying: "Now...it's my turn."

Acknowledgments

Kingdom Building Ministries offers a heartfelt thanks to all those who helped to compile the information in this book. Many people spent countless hours researching, writing and editing. We could not have produced this book without their tireless dedication. Our prayer is that God would be glorified in your life through their efforts.

Why is it my turn now?

Relay races are won or lost at the hand-off of the baton.

In the same way, Christianity has survived nearly two thousand years as the result of millions of successful transfers of the baton. Christ handed off his message of new life and servanthood to his disciples. They, in turn, handed it off to a few thousand believers. Those thousands went out to spread the "good news" to the entire known world during the first century.

But the message would have been lost, if it was not also passed on from generation to generation, century to century. Now, it's our turn. The baton is in our hands! Will *we* carry Christ's message into the next century?

A Biblical Perspective

This book is about fifteen faithful "runners" who not only passed on their faith, but lived it out in a real, vital manner. Living out one's faith—in front of those around us—is the effective method Christ and his disciples have used down through the centuries. It's called "mentoring." The Apostle Paul demonstrates this principle when he writes to the believers in Corinth. "Therefore I urge you to imitate me" (1 Corinthians 4:16). Later in this same letter, Paul writes, "Follow my example, as I follow the example of Christ" (1 Corinthians 11:1).

The writer of Hebrews recognized the power of historical mentors or role models. In the eleventh chapter of Hebrews, following the definition of faith, we have one of the most amazing lists in the Bible. These heroes of faith, both named and unnamed, serve as ongoing illustrations of the benefits of selling out to God and taking the risk of faith. Chapter twelve continues with an exhortation to persevere, reminding us of the great cloud of witnesses who have gone before us.

But the real power of historical mentoring is captured in an often misunderstood paragraph in the final chapter of the book of Hebrews. "Remember your leaders, who spoke the word of God to you. Consider the outcome of their way of life and imitate their faith" (Hebrews 13:7).

Wrapped up in this commonly overlooked verse are three very practical applications that relate to the subject of heroes, role models, and historical mentors.

> *Often we are tempted to imitate the actions of our heroes. But God has a race marked out just for you.*

First, we are told to *"Remember your leaders."* Many of today's young adults have a fragmented or disjointed view of history. Too often we fail to see ourselves as part of an ongoing wave in the sea of humanity. We view today as an isolated moment in time rather than a continuation of God's sovereign plan to reconcile the world to Himself. This interruption in the unfolding saga of history keeps us from relating meaningfully to the great heroes of faith who have gone before us. We have robbed ourselves of some of the most powerful role models and mentors we could ever hope to have.

Imagine it! The greatest heroes of the Christian faith are waiting on the shelves of a bookstore or library for the opportunity to share with you the secrets of doing great things for God. During the heat of their battle, only a handful of people could get close to them. Most great leaders have a fairly small network of inner confidants who spend time with them, share their heart, and participate in their struggles of faith. But we can unobtrusively enter into their lives. We can read entries from their journals, sit in their board meetings and observe them in their most vulnerable moments—if we would but remember our leaders.

Second, we are challenged to *"Consider the outcome of their way of life."* Many of the sacrifices on the road to greatness in God's eyes are only brought into perspective when viewed from the end looking back. This hindsight perspective is to life what a scale is to a map. It brings a sense of balance to our journey and helps us process the difficulties along the way.

A classic illustration of this truth comes from the life of an historical mentor named C.T. Studd. Born in the 1800's, he grew up in a wealthy family in England and made a name for himself through his athletic ability playing cricket (the British version of baseball). He shocked the world of cricket by heeding the call of Hudson Taylor and sailing for China as a missionary. While in China, this twenty-five year old missionary received final confirmation of the inheritance he knew would be coming from his father's fortune. By today's standards, C.T. Studd was independently wealthy. He would never need to work or raise support again.

He had prayed much about his inheritance and was convinced God wanted him to seize the golden opportunity of doing what the rich young ruler had failed to do. On January 13, 1887, C.T. Studd gave away his fortune. In the eyes of man he was a fool. But consider the outcome of his way of life.

He gave 5,000 British pounds to D.L. Moody, an evangelist who had been instrumental in the conversion of his father. Moody took that money and began a training center in the city of Chicago, now known as Moody Bible Institute. C.T. sent another 5,000 pounds to George Mueller, who was doing extraordinary work among orphans in England. He sent a total of 8,400 pounds to the Salvation Army, an organization working among the outcasts of London and beyond. The list goes on of the people and ministries that God blessed through this twenty-five year old missionary to China. Only eternity will give the final outcome of this one act of sacrificial obedience in C.T. Studd's way of life.

Third, we are reminded to *"Imitate their faith."* Notice we are not exhorted to imitate their lives. We are told to imitate their *faith.* Often we are tempted to imitate the actions of our heroes. But God has a race marked out just for you. It is the faith, not the actions, of others that is worthy of our imitation.

It's our turn

Remember your leaders. Consider the outcome of their way of life. Imitate their faith. These are powerful admonitions. But the real force of these truths turns on the very next verse. "Jesus Christ is the same yesterday and today and forever" (Hebrews 13:8).

You have probably heard that verse quoted many times. But rarely is it ever placed in its true context. Verses seven and eight of Hebrews thirteen make up one complete paragraph. They are connected by one common thought. The entire point of verse eight is to emphasize that what God has done in the lives of great leaders who have gone before us, He is still prepared to do through people like you today!

> *What God has done in the lives of great leaders. . .He is still prepared to do through people like you today!*

We are called to live lives of purity, obedience, sacrifice and faith. But we are not alone. We are surrounded by a great cloud of witnesses who have modeled for us this life of faith. As we remember them, consider the outcome of their way of life, and imitate their faith. With our lives we write new chapters for future generations who will follow in our footsteps. It's our turn!

In the following pages you will read biographical sketches of laborers who have gone before us. Some of these leaders will spark within you a passion to learn more from the Kingdom exploits for which they are noted. For this reason, we have included a suggested biography for further reading. We have also included fifteen characteristics that exemplified these laborers — characteristics that we can imitate to become faithful laborers ourselves. In this way, you'll be mentored by these great leaders and laborers.

Take the time to interact with these laborers. You will find their lives thought-provoking. Write down your responses in both the *application* and *journal response* sections. These interaction sections are designed to assist you in summarizing your next steps in obedience to God.

You may wish to dig deeper into the lives of these historical mentors by reading a full biography about them. We have suggested additional reading material after each chapter.

One of the best ways to fully grasp new truth is to teach it to someone else. You may even consider using this book as a resource for small group interaction. Or you may wish to seek out a contemporary mentor from whom you can learn as you read. Mentoring is a powerful relational stimulus for spiritual growth. You will be facing some serious issues as you walk through this material. The encouragement, counsel and accountability of a mentor will be invaluable.

Finally, make a commitment to be a laborer. This book will challenge you to make a decision. You will have the opportunity to affirm your desire to become a laborer in God's harvest field by signing *The Laborer's Declaration.* As you look over the affirmations in *The Laborer's Declaration,* remember the words of Solomon who said, "it is better not to make a vow than to make one and not keep it." Be sure you are motivated by a sincere desire to press on as a laborer by the grace of God before you sign *The Laborer's Declaration.* If you do, let us know by returning the enclosed business reply card. We will send you some helpful information as a means of supporting your commitment.

Remember, *"It's my turn."*

DECLARATION 1:

It's my turn to die to self.

Amy Carmichael

(1867-1951)

Seventeen-year-old Amy Carmichael was on her way home from church in Belfast, when she came a poor old woman carrying a heavy bundle-something she was not accustomed to seeing in Presbyterian Belfast. Amy, along with her two brothers, took the bundle from the woman and helped her along by the arms.

Surrounded by the "respectable people" of the community, Amy could not help but notice her actions were being questioned. She was embarrassed. In her own words Amy described it as "a horrid moment. We were only two boys and a girl, and not at all exalted Christians. We hated doing it." They plodded on in spite of the blushing and sense of shame for associating publicly with such a woman. The wind and rain blew in their faces. The rags of the old woman pressed against them.

Just as they passed by an ornate Victorian fountain in the street, "this mighty phrase flashed as it were through the gray drizzle: 'Gold, silver, precious stones, wood, hay stubble—every man's work will be made manifest; for the day shall declare it, because it shall be declared by fire; and the fire shall try every man's work of what sort it is. If any man's work abide...'"

The words were so real, Amy turned to see who had spoken them. She saw nothing but a muddy street, people with surprised looks on their faces, and the fountain. But Amy knew this was the voice of God.

That afternoon, Amy shut the door to her room and closed

herself in with God. What happened that day would change the course of her life and profoundly impact her priorities. Amy Carmichael began to understand what it means to die to self.

How did this affect her? She purposed in her heart to follow Him who had no home, no earthly possessions beyond the bare minimum. She would be "dead to the world and its applause, to all its customs, fashions, laws." Amy had an eye for beauty and it was no small sacrifice to embrace this journey of true discipleship.

Amy began to reach out to the "shawlies," girls who worked in the mills and were too poor to buy hats. They used their shawls to cover their heads, which was offensive to the proper church members. Which was worse, Amy bringing these crude "commoners" to the church or Mrs. Carmichael allowing her to go into the slums to fetch them? They couldn't decide.

> *A crucified life cannot be self-assertive. The cup that is full of sweet water cannot spill bitter-tasting drops, however sharply it is knocked.*
>
> *Amy Carmichael*

Amy didn't care about her reputation. She was dead. Christ was alive in her, loving the shawlies through her. It was a relief to the church folk when the shawlies were coming in such large numbers that Amy needed a separate building for them. This was no small challenge for a now 22-year-old girl. But Amy believed God for both the land and the building. The invitations were sent out and the grand opening set for January 2, 1889. She invited her minister to dedicate "The Mill and Factory Girls' Branch of the YWCA." A banner was hung in the front with the words, "That in all things He might have the preeminence."

Two students of D. L. Moody led the service. Amy wasn't on the platform that night. She wasn't on the program. Yes, it was her vision that initiated the ministry and her dream that brought about the building. But she sat inconspicuously in the middle of the audience. Amy Carmichael had died to self.

Later, when God called Amy to missions, she did not question, though it saddened her to leave her loved ones. On the mission field, God again used Amy's "mother's heart" to minister to children. She spent fifty-three years in India setting up orphanages to rescue children from prostitution in Hindu temples and ministering to the people she met. Amy affected the lives of countless Indians, giving them a hope for a future on earth and in heaven.

While serving in India, Amy received a letter from a young lady who was considering life as a missionary. She asked Amy, "What is missionary life like?" Amy wrote back saying simply, "Missionary life is a chance to die."

Significant Contribution

Amy's life and ministry exemplifies the heart of the Father who embraces the orphans, widows and outcasts of society. Like Queen Esther, God used Amy to rescue the lives of thousands, by giving her a role only a godly woman could fulfill.

Recommended Reading

A Chance to Die, The Life and Legacy of Amy Carmichael, by Elisabeth Elliot

APPLICATION

1. At one point in her early years Amy said, "Nothing could ever matter again but the things that were eternal." Nothing? What is your response to that?

2. In 1886, Amy was gripped by Jude 24. What does it say to you?

3. As a youngster, Amy rejected the dark brown eyes God had given her, and longed instead for blue eyes. But with her brown eyes, she was later able to go inside the Hindu temples to rescue children. Is there any unchangeable feature of your own body (God's design) that you reject? Thank God for it, instead.

4. Amy demonstrated death to self by praying for money without telling anyone. Is there a sum of money for a specific ministry you could ask only God to provide?

5. One night, Amy led her oxcart driver to Christ. Later, she found out that a group of prayer warriors back home had been praying specifically on that date for a convert to be won. Pause right now and pray for a missionary.

6. After Amy's book sales had passed the half million mark in fifteen languages and Braille, she learned that a magazine article had described her books as popular. She responded, "Popular? Lord, is that what these books written out of the heat of the battle are? Popular? O Lord, burn the paper to ashes if that be true." What does it mean to have a "single eye" for the glory of God?

JOURNAL RESPONSE

1. What did I learn from this historical mentor? (Character trait, truth, life principle or method?)

2. How do I feel about applying this to my life? (Challenged, frightened, liberated, stimulated?)

3. What next step should I take in response? (My personal application of this truth or principle.)

4. Who could encourage me and hold me accountable? (Friend, mentor, pastor, parent, etc.)

5. Why is this lesson important for me today? (How will this enable me to build God's Kingdom?)

DECLARATION 2:

It's my turn to embrace God through worship.

Keith Green

(1954-1982)

The life of Keith Green brings together a unique blend of musical genius, spiritual destiny, and uncompromising commitment. After finding his way through the maze of values that were so common in the late sixties and early seventies, Keith poured his life into challenging the church to move beyond the complacent norms of religious institutions. His message was fiery and at times controversial. But his heart radiated an unyielding passion for Jesus, and his music stands today as a testimony of his single-minded love.

Keith Green was constantly striving for a deeper, more intimate relationship with his Lord. Out of this desire, and Keith's personal time with God, came many choruses and songs of worship. "O Lord, You're Beautiful," was the result of one such occasion. "The Lord brought me right into the throne room, and I sang to Him and just worshipped," said Keith about the song. Keith's heart and passion are wrapped into the lyrics:

O Lord, You're beautiful. Your face is all I seek.
For when Your eyes are on this child, Your grace abounds to me...

Keith was never content to be mediocre about anything. His

music reflected his excellence, but more clearly spoke of his relationship with his Lord. Nothing was dearer to him than knowing God personally.

Worship to Keith meant more than singing a few choruses and offering a few prayers. It was a constant need, that was reflected in everything he did. Out of this relationship, sprang the desire to serve God and to see others truly worship, to develop the same intimacy with his Lord that Keith was realizing.

While Keith was a quickly rising star on the Christian music scene, he felt God calling him to present a concert, or series of evenings in Tulsa, on the Oral Roberts University campus. With permission from the ORU administration to hold three evening programs, Keith began his preparations. The first two evenings were successful, if the number of persons responding to Keith's message was any indication. Keith, however, was not satisfied, believing God was going to move more powerfully in Tulsa and bring a city-wide revival.

> *"We alone have the commission, the power, and the truth of God at our constant disposal to deliver sinner after sinner from eternal death."*
>
> **Keith Green**

The third evening, the Mabee Center was packed with about 4,500 people. Many had heard of the happenings of the last two evenings. Keith had fasted and prayed all day, listening for the message God wanted presented that night.

After opening with praises, worship and welcoming the presence of God, what Keith brought to the meeting was a list of sins God had told him were present on the campus. He challenged the audience to confess their sins, reminding them of the pain they were causing Christ. A flood of individuals streamed forward to kneel or prostrate themselves before God at the front, in the aisles, or as close as they could get. As they came, Keith played the piano, not watching to see what was happening, but looking up and concentrating on God. He tearfully called for God to send His Spirit to break the hearts of everyone present.

Keith opened the microphone to anyone who had something they felt they needed to confess. Many threaded their way down the people-packed aisles to the front, and a line soon formed at the microphone. Admissions of not supporting the ORU administration, false Christianity and breaking curfew led to emotional confessions of taking drugs, sexual misconduct and homosexuality. With each confession came a deeper and more overwhelming sense of the nearness of the Spirit of God in the auditorium.

Keith, meanwhile, had crawled under the piano, in order to not interfere with the moving of the Spirit, and to worship and praise God for His presence. Keith, in his times of worship and relationship with his Lord had indeed heard Him correctly. Revival came to Tulsa as a result of Keith's obedience and service born out of worship.

In addition to his music, Keith became a prophetic speaker and author, sharing his passion with the body of Christ in articles and tracts published through Last Days Ministries, the organization he founded with his wife, Melody. In what seemed to be the prime of his life, Keith, and two of his children, were killed in a tragic plane crash. His vision lives on and his influence will be felt for generations to come.

Significant Contribution

Keith's public ministry through writing, teaching and music challenged the Church to go beyond spiritual apathy, embracing a total surrender to God. He surrendered his talents and gifts to God, later using the vehicle of music to challenge his generation to reach the world.

Recommended Reading

No Compromise, by Melody Green and David Hazard

APPLICATION

1. Read Psalms 149 and 150. Notice the diverse styles of worship. What is the most effective way you have found to worship God?

2. How does the Apostle Paul suggest we worship in Colossians 3:1-17? What conditions are necessary?

3. Keith Green said, "With almost every promise in the Bible comes a condition." What "conditions" are essential for knowing God intimately?

4. Shortly before he was killed, Green was sending free subscriptions of Last Days Newsletter to 300,000 people and giving away his best-selling albums. If we are in a spiritual war, consider the analogy of armies not charging their own soldiers for ammunition. How much should ministries charge Christians for publications? (Soldiers do pay taxes.) By what principles can ministries determine how to finance the materials they distribute?

How do you determine to which ministries you will make donations?

JOURNAL RESPONSE

1. What did I learn from this historical mentor? (Character trait, truth, life principle or method?)

2. How do I feel about applying this to my life? (Challenged, frightened, liberated, stimulated?)

3. What next step should I take in response? (My personal application of this truth or principle.)

4. Who could encourage me and hold me accountable? (Friend, mentor, pastor, parent, etc.)

5. Why is this lesson important for me today? (How will this enable me to build God's Kingdom?)

It's my turn to intercede for the lost.

John Hyde

(1865-1912)

Just before the turn of the 20th century John Hyde sensed a call to go to an unreached people group in the nation of India. He ministered in the Punjab, and was one of only five missionaries to serve in that whole region.

He was slow of speech, slightly hearing impaired, and thought to lack the enthusiasm and zeal a young missionary should have. Hyde neglected his language study for a time in order to study the Bible. When reprimanded by his committee, he simply said, "First things first." Results were meager, and showed no signs of improvement. Conversions were rare in that part of the world among national workers, much less foreigners.

It was at this point that John Hyde determined he was going to have to lean on the power of prayer. He began to lead his fellow missionaries in intercession for the nation of India. In 1899, he began spending entire nights in prayer! He would work all day, then labor in prayer all night.

Prayer for the lost became his passion, and his sole, "secret weapon" for ministry. In 1904, he attended an annual convention where Indian Christians and local missionaries met together. In this meeting, the Punjab Prayer Union was formed under the leadership of John Hyde. He convinced the workers that nothing was going to happen for the Kingdom of God apart from intercessory prayer. So little fruit had been borne to any of those workers, that it didn't take much to convince them of this truth.

In 1908, Hyde dared to pray for what many considered an impossible request. He asked God for one soul per day to be won to Christ. That would mean 365 before the next convention! Although most could not fathom such results, they let Hyde go on with his gigantic request—and by the next convention, over 400 had been won to Christ!

During that 1909 convention, Hyde presented his next prayer goal. He wanted to double the number of souls won—two souls per day. It seemed impossible again, but this time, his fellow workers joined him in prayer. Sure enough, by the next convention, over 800 souls had been won! In that convention, he determined to double the goal again. He prayed with almost violent passion: "Give me souls or I die!" Four souls a day was the goal that was set and met, and it was at this time, that John received his now famous nickname:

> *"O, God, give me souls or I die!"*
>
> *John Hyde*

"Praying Hyde". He began to travel about, igniting other workers and nationals to pray for the lost in India.

It was while he was in Calcutta that some friends noticed his failing health. They talked him into seeing a doctor, but no one expected the incredible discovery made by this doctor. John "Praying" Hyde's heart had actually shifted positions inside his body. It was now over on the left side of his chest! Evidently, the years of passionate "labor" in both prayer and calling others to prayer had effected his frail, human body. The doctor gave stern instructions that he must get total rest for weeks or he would die. But "Praying Hyde" could not see letting up, and he continued his passionate ministry of intercession. He went on to live two more years, and saw a wave of conversions come in that had never been seen before in that part of the world. Today, John "Praying" Hyde stands as a testimony, not so much of gifts and intellect, but of the results that come when we simply intercede.

Significant Contribution

Hyde's missionary methods underscore the truth that prayer is the driving force behind world evangelization. Like the early apostles, John Hyde recognized that time in prayer and study of the scriptures could not be compromised by other seemingly worthwhile activities.

Recommended Reading

John Hyde, by Francis McGraw

APPLICATION

1. At age seventeen, Hyde discovered that the purpose of prayer is not to get from God what we want, but to allow God to receive from us what He wants. What does He want from you?

2. At age twenty-seven Hyde faced an unexpected giant that threatened to destroy the effectiveness of his prayer life: pride of spiritual achievement. What does 1 Corinthians 4:7 say about the things you are tempted to call your accomplishments?

3. In Bombay, Hyde discovered that in spite of his seminary training, he did not really know the Bible. Shortly thereafter he adjusted his schedule in order to master God's Word, in spite of giving less time to language study. The villagers came to his defense saying, "He speaks the language of our hearts." What connection(s) do you see between Hyde's increased study of the Bible and his connection with the hearts of the people?

4.   Sometimes Hyde would go into a village and find that some of the believers were quarreling or had slipped back into idolatry. He would call the group together, but instead of rebuking or exhorting them, he would ask everyone to pray. He would remain before the group, kneeling or often on his face, mostly in silence for two or three hours. What do you think was at work here: a method, or a Person?

5.   Another lesson Hyde learned about persistent prayer—spending all night in prayer. Have you ever attempted it? See Luke 6:12.

6.   Hyde believed God wanted him to ask for one soul per day. He recorded 400 conversions that year. The next year he asked for two per day and won over 800. The next year he asked God for four per day, and God was faithful. Do you think God is directing you to set a soul-winning goal?

JOURNAL RESPONSE

1. What did I learn from this historical mentor? (Character trait, truth, life principle or method?)

2. How do I feel about applying this to my life? (Challenged, frightened, liberated, stimulated?)

3. What next step should I take in response? (My personal application of this truth or principle.)

4. Who could encourage me and hold me accountable? (Friend, mentor, pastor, parent, etc.)

5. Why is this lesson important for me today? (How will this enable me to build God's Kingdom?)

DECLARATION 4:

It's my turn to sacrifice for the cause of Christ.

C.T. Studd

(1862-1931)

At fifty years of age, C.T. Studd was not the prime candidate for a frontier missions thrust to the heart of unevangelized Africa. At least not from a human point of view. He had already served in China and India. Along with Stanley Smith, Studd led the Cambridge Seven in 1885 as missionaries to China with the China Inland Mission. He also toured the universities of America in the early stages of the Student Volunteer Movement, a student movement that mobilized more than 20,000 career missionaries! His health had been a hindrance for fifteen years. His severe asthma alone was reason enough to keep him out of tropical Africa, but God had a plan.

In Liverpool in 1908, C.T. noticed a sign that piqued his sense of humor and curiosity. "Cannibals want missionaries." *Why, sure they do, for more reasons than one,* C.T. said to himself. He was hooked. He had to go in and hear more.

Dr. Karl Krumm, who had walked across Africa, was telling his experiences. Karl Krumm explained that in the middle of the continent there were numbers of tribes who had never heard the story of Jesus Christ. Explorers had been to those regions, big-game hunters, traders, European officials and scientists, but no Christian had ever gone to tell of Jesus.

"The shame sank deep into one's soul." C.T. said, "Why have

no Christians gone?" God replied, "Why don't you go?" "The doctors won't permit it," he said. The answer came, "Am I not the Good Physician? Can I not take you through? Can I not keep you there?" There were no excuses, it had to be done.

But how was he to do it? He was in ill health. He had no money. He was already beyond the prime of his life. None of this would deter him. C.T. discussed a strategy with Karl Krumm. They agreed on a plan to make an exploratory journey to the Southern Sudan, a thousand miles south of Khartoum. The rapid spread of Islam gave them both a sense of urgency to plant a chain of mission stations to stem the tide.

Then came the need for funding. C.T. outlined the challenge and explained he was willing to lead the charge. God rallied a group of businessmen who were willing to back the project. They presented one important qualifier. C.T. must see a doctor and be given a medical clearance.

> *"Some wish to live within the sound of church or chapel bell, I want to run a rescue shop within a yard of hell."*
>
> ## *C.T. Studd*

The doctor told them C.T. would die if he ventured south of Khartoum. He must agree to this precondition or there would be no funds. C.T. could never comply with this kind of limitation. It would undermine the entire project. He responded to the group of businessmen with these words, "Gentlemen, God has called me to go, and I will go. I will blaze the trail, though my grave may only become a stepping stone that younger man may follow."

It was insane. A penniless fifty year old man with asthma and malaria bent on going to the heart of Africa. But C.T. had learned that God laughs at impossibilities. His years of service under the leadership of Hudson Taylor and the China Inland Mission had proven in the crucible of life that God could be trusted. He would proceed by faith.

"God sent supplies in a wonderful way" C.T. exclaimed. The result? He went on the exploratory mission and while in Sudan, C.T. was told about masses of people in the Belgian Congo who had never heard of Christ. They were in desperate need. That settled it. He would never be able to spend the remainder of his years in England.

The exploratory mission came to a close, and C.T. returned to England aflame with a vision for this New Crusade. He traveled to Cambridge and gave an impassioned plea on behalf of the unreached peoples in the heart of Africa. He also wrote powerful booklets like *The Shame of Christ* and *The Chocolate Soldier* that fueled the fires of his cause. He outlined the basic principles upon which the mission would be built.

Then it was back to Africa. The night before he left, C.T. spoke with a young man who questioned his plans. "Is it a fact that at fifty-two you mean to leave your country, your home, your wife and your children?" In a flash of inspiration C.T. responded, "If Jesus Christ be God and died for me, then no sacrifice can be too great for me to make for Him." It would become the motto of the crusade.

The doctor was right. C.T. Studd died in Africa. Twenty years later! Through his faith and obedience in the face of great sacrifice, many thousands were brought into the Kingdom and a new mission agency (WEC International) was born. His last written words were: "Let God be magnified! Hallelujah!"

Significant Contribution

One of the fruits of C.T. Studd's radical obedience was the formation of Heart of Africa Mission. Later known as WEC International (Worldwide Evangelization Crusade), Heart of Africa Mission was a new agency birthed out of his pioneer ministry among the unreached peoples of central Africa. Not only was C.T. a model laborer, he also became an influential mobilizer challenging thousands of students to join him on the front lines of the battle.

Recommended Reading

C.T. Studd, Cricketer and Pioneer, by Norman Grubb

APPLICATION

1. As a young missionary in China, C.T. learned that his recently deceased father had left him the equivalent of $150,000. Having just finished reading Jesus' advice to the rich young man to "go thy way, sell all you have and give to the poor, and you will have treasure in heaven," he immediately decided to do likewise. His gifts were instrumental in the establishment of Moody Bible Institute, George Mueller's ministry to orphans, and the Salvation Army. What do you have that you should give to a ministry?

2. At age fifty, with no money, and after fifteen years of illness, C.T. responded to the call to go to Africa. What is retirement, and should Christians do it? Explain.

3. C.T. spent his boyhood in a spacious mansion, but died dwelling in a stick hut in the jungle. Moses "esteemed the reproach of Christ greater than the treasures of Egypt." In prayer, give to God your expectations about a dwelling.

4.   C.T. said, "How could I spend the best years of my life in living for the honours of this world, when thousands of souls are perishing every day?" Today, do something to rescue the perishing. Write down what it will be.

5.   Among C.T.'s correspondence was this quote, "Remember that mere soul-saving is comparatively easy work, and is not nearly so important as that of manufacturing the saved ones into Saints, Soldiers and Saviours." Put that into your own words.

JOURNAL RESPONSE

1.   What did I learn from this historical mentor? (Character trait, truth, life principle or method?)

2.   How do I feel about applying this to my life? (Challenged, frightened, liberated, stimulated?)

3.   What next step should I take in response? (My personal application of this truth or principle.)

4.   Who could encourage me and hold me accountable? (Friend, mentor, pastor, parent, etc.)

5.   Why is this lesson important for me today? (How will this enable me to build God's Kingdom?)

DECLARATION 5:

It's my turn to share the Gospel.

D.L. Moody

(1837-1899)

One of the greatest models of lifestyle evangelism comes from the life of Dwight Moody. This is true not only because Moody was committed to communicating the Gospel of Jesus Christ to lost people on a regular basis, but because he did so without possessing any unusual gifts or abilities to do so.

Mr. Kimball, an ordinary shoe salesman and Dwight's Sunday School teacher, was committed to making sure every boy and girl in his class had an opportunity to hear, understand and respond to the message of Christ. He took a special interest in Dwight, and shared with him one afternoon during the week. His message, his love, and his lifestyle were all compelling— and soon, young Dwight had asked Jesus Christ to be the Lord of his life.

Dwight Moody never forgot that experience. He figured if an ordinary, common shoe clerk could have that kind of impact on kids—so could he. Consequently, as a young adult, Moody began his own ministry to children. He would gather them from the streets and the docks around Chicago and tell them the stories of the Bible. Often, it was latch-key kids who had no one to watch over them in the afternoons that would respond so quickly. Moody used to bring them to church in large groups. His church would frequently have campaigns where church members would "rent" space in the pews for guests or family members. Moody would pay for entire pews to bring his young converts. Despite the fact that he failed to pass ordination requirements early in his ministry, Dwight continued in his determination to minister to both kids and adults who didn't know Christ.

Two significant events happened during his ministry that drove him in his evangelistic efforts. One happened in 1817, during an evangelistic service. Moody was preaching one night on how God desired everyone to repent and be saved. Since it was a series of meetings on the subject, Moody told them to return the next evening for an opportunity to respond to the Gospel message. That opportunity never came for many in that audience. It was on that night that the great Chicago fire broke out, and hundreds lost their lives, including many who heard Moody preach that evening. Dwight was devastated. He determined that he would never again miss a chance to compel people to respond immediately to the message of the Gospel.

> *"Before my conversion I worked toward the cross, but since then I have worked from the cross; then I worked to be saved, now I work because I am saved."*
>
> **D.L. Moody**

The second turning point came after Moody was filled with the Holy Spirit. While in New York, God surprised him by coming upon him in great power. Moody had been filled and began to notice the difference in his ministry. He said his "sermons were no different, but now hundreds were being saved" after he preached. It was at this time that Moody set a goal for himself. He determined that he was going to win someone to Christ every day for the rest of his life, God willing. He wrote this commitment down in his journal, and by his own admission said he kept it "even if he didn't get any sleep at night." He won someone daily to Christ! Moody was a man who was committed to see what God could do with one whose life was totally surrendered to Him. In the course of his work, Moody established three Christian schools, a publishing business, a Christian conference, and a

Bible institute. He also was instrumental in inspiring preachers to win souls through revivals.

It is also reputed that Moody traveled a million miles, preached to 100 million people, and won a million souls to Christ. Moody chose to center his ministry in Chicago and to focus it primarily on the worst sections of the city, believing no one else would care to reach these people. Perhaps the greatest tribute to and reason for Moody's success is that in every sense of the word, he was a man of prayer.

Having personally won a million souls for Christ, Dwight Moody stands as a model witness for us today.

Significant Contribution

In spite of his lack of formal training, Moody did more to reach his generation for Christ than any other layman. Through popularizing the Sunday School and the use of crusade evangelism, he personally introduced more than one million souls to Christ.

Recommended Reading

D.L. Moody, The Greatest Evangelist of the Nineteenth Century, by Faith Coxe Bailey

APPLICATION

1. Moody and a friend started a Sunday School in an abandoned boxcar. If creativity is seeing what others have overlooked, ask God to give you one creative observation that would help in reaching someone with the Gospel.

2. Henry Varley, a preacher friend, casually remarked, "The world has yet to see what God will do with a man fully consecrated to Him." After pondering those words for weeks, Moody resolved that by the Holy Spirit's power, he would be that man. Put yourself in Moody's shoes; would you make the same resolution?

3. In order to respond to God's call to the ministry, Moody's earnings dropped from $5,000 per year to $150 per year. Look over one month's check register in search of money that could be given to God's work.

4.   Even though Moody spoke to over one and a half million people during a two year campaign in London, he refused to allow a tallying of the number of conversions. He also refused money "all the time," saying, "I am not going to give any man ground for saying that we're making a gain out of preaching the gospel." List a few important guidelines for record keeping that ministers and ministries should employ.

5.   As he watched 200 young men of Cambridge respond to the gospel, Moody said, "My God, this is enough to live for." Can you put into a single sentence what you are living for?

What would an objective observer say you are living for?

JOURNAL RESPONSE

1. What did I learn from this historical mentor? (Character trait, truth, life principle or method?)

2. How do I feel about applying this to my life? (Challenged, frightened, liberated, stimulated?)

3. What next step should I take in response? (My personal application of this truth or principle.)

4. Who could encourage me and hold me accountable? (Friend, mentor, pastor, parent, etc.)

5. Why is this lesson important for me today? (How will this enable me to build God's Kingdom?)

DECLARATION 6:

It's my turn to stand for what is true and right.

Martin Luther

(1483-1546)

The offer to recant, to take back all the things he had said and written, must have been tempting for Martin Luther as he stood before the Diet of Worms in April of 1521. After all, Luther was just a common monk. How had he come to be before Charles V, the emperor of Germany, being tried for treason and heresy? As a monk and a priest in the Roman Catholic church, Luther wearied his priest with confessions, constant scathing self examinations and personal punishments, stemming from a concern that he was not forgiven for his sins. Romans 1:17 turned Luther's life around when he realized that salvation is by faith alone, not by works, as was the teaching of his time.

As his understanding and theology developed, Luther became concerned with the materialistic corruption, legalism and lack of spiritual care in the church. From this concern Luther wrote his *95 Theses* and tacked it to the church door in Wittenburg, Germany. This was not a rebellious or radical action, but the traditional method of inviting discussion on an issue. However, from his *Theses* and subsequent writings, the Reformation movement was born.

Following the posting of his *95 Theses* on the door of the Wittenburg church in 1517, Luther continued to write and speak for reform within the Catholic Church. His ideas rapidly gained approval among the common people of Germany, who were frustrated with the lack of spiritual care, materialistic corruption and political maneuvering of the Church. In all this controversy, Luther never viewed himself as a rebel, but merely as fulfilling his vow to teach and defend the scriptures.

Luther pointed to 1518 as the year of his conversion. By then he had already been a monk for over ten years, devoted to the study and teaching of scripture and to prayer. It was in 1518 that the simplicity of Romans 1:17 became apparent to him. In this scripture he found that the righteousness demanded of God in the law is provided through faith in Jesus Christ alone. The only requirement was faith to receive the perfect righteousness of Christ as atonement for sin.

"I own but one thing, my own unworthy body. . .If they choose to take it. . .they will but make me poorer by one or two hours of life. The sweet Redeemer, my Lord Jesus Christ, is enough for me, to whom I shall sing as long as I live. And if anyone is unwilling to sing with me, then what is that to me."

Martin Luther

In 1520 Luther wrote three treatises while facing increased pressure from Pope Leo X to recant under the threat of excommunication. The first, "To the Christian Nobility of the German Nation," appealed for the German secular leaders to call a council to implement reforms within the Church. Included was a list of items for the a council to consider, such as restraints on the role of the Pope in the Church and the sale of indulgences.

Luther's second treatise "The Babylonian Captivity of the Church," dealt with the use of the sacraments. In it, Luther rejected five of the seven sacraments and the priestly order within the church. To Luther, every believer served as a priest.

The third treatise, "On the Freedom of the Christian," held that justification and the forgiveness of sins came through faith alone. The Church had associated forgiveness with laws, rules, politics and the purchase of indulgences.

By January of 1521 Luther was an outlaw of the Holy Roman Empire and had been excommunicated by the Church. About the same time, Emperor Charles V was calling for the imperial diet (trial) to meet at Worms to determine Luther's fate.

As the diet began, Luther was shown a large pile of books and asked, "Did you write these books?" After stating that he had, Luther was asked, "Will you now take back all the things you said in these books?" He asked for time to consider the question, and the emperor allowed him one day to respond.

The next day the meeting was moved to a larger hall, but still the crowd could not squeeze in. Luther was asked the question again. Although the exact words of his reply have been debated, he is reported to have said, "Unless I am convinced, by scripture or by plain reason...I cannot and will not recant. It is neither safe nor right to go against one's conscience. Here I stand. I cannot do otherwise. God help me." His statement sent shockwaves through the audience as the listeners added their own opinions to the chaos.

The fear of revolt by the people of Germany led even the strongest opposers of Luther to appeal to the emperor for a continued private hearing by a committee. Three days of questioning and appeals for Luther to change his stand were unsuccessful. He would not be moved.

Later, Luther would write that the thought which consumed him during those interviews was not that he was before an emperor, but rather that both of them would need to answer before God. The desire to stand unashamed before his heavenly Father gave him strength to stand unwavering before the earthly emperor. God's Word was Luther's final authority.

Significant Contribution

Martin Luther's *95 Theses*, tacked to the Wittenburg Chapel door, summarized his protest against the Roman Catholic Church and ushered in the Protestant Reformation of the early sixteenth century.

Recommended Reading

The Luther Legacy, by George Wolfgang Forell

APPLICATION

1.   What does Romans 1:17 say to you?

2.   Luther faced criticism for his teaching of *sola fides* (faith alone), *sola gratia* (grace alone), and *solus Christus* (Christ alone). What does Ephesians 2:8-9 say to you?

3.   At his trial, Luther said, "Unless I am convinced by the testimony of Scripture or by clear reason (for I trust neither Pope nor council alone, since it is well known that they have often erred and contradicted themselves), I am bound by the Scriptures I have cited, for my conscience is captive to the Word of God. I cannot and will not recant anything, since to act against one's conscience is neither safe nor right. I cannot do otherwise. Here I stand, may God help me." What do you think contributed to his resolve?

4. Rate yourself on the following scale.

    I give up at the   1 2 3 4 5 6 7 8 9 10   *I persevere*
    drop of a hat.   *to the end.*

5. Read Romans 5:3-6. What factors help build endurance?

6. Write a brief prayer, telling God of your intention to be an individual of conviction.

JOURNAL RESPONSE

1. What did I learn from this historical mentor? (Character trait, truth, life principle or method?)

2. How do I feel about applying this to my life? (Challenged, frightened, liberated, stimulated?)

3. What next step should I take in response? (My personal application of this truth or principle.)

4. Who could encourage me and hold me accountable? (Friend, mentor, pastor, parent, etc.)

5. Why is this lesson important for me today? (How will this enable me to build God's Kingdom?)

DECLARATION 7:

It's my turn to live by faith.

George Mueller

(1805-1898)

Before he was twenty, none would have believed that George Mueller would become a great man of faith working with orphans in England. However, this is exactly what took place in Mueller's life as God changed him and used him.

Although he was raised and confirmed in the church, Mueller lived his life denying the reality of God. Mueller became widely known for his thievery and drunkenness, even stealing from his own father. Then to everyone's surprise, God took hold of Mueller's life and began a wondrous work. When he was twenty, Mueller became involved in a prayer meeting that led not only to his salvation, but also to a realization of God's calling on his life.

Although a widely traveled man, he based his extensive ministry in Bristol, England. Mueller was a visionary who did not know how to think small. Consequently, when he caught his burden to care for and minister to orphans in Great Britain, he was determined to do it right. He prayed long hours. He fasted. He began to share his burden and vision with others, who could partner with him in some way. Soon the buildings grew. Some were built, some were bought—but eventually whole city blocks of facilities were owned by Mueller's Orphanage which housed, fed and taught homeless children. It was a tribute to God and to what faith could do.

Throughout the remainder of his life, Mueller lived totally by faith, not accepting wages or borrowing money. He believed that God would provide whatever was needed, and Mueller was never disappointed.

A very common story in his ministry stemmed from meal times. Because the ministry was run completely by faith, they seldom had huge stockpiles of food. Numerous times the staff would have the children sit down at the dining hall tables without any food in the kitchen at all. It almost seemed ludicrous. With nothing to serve, they still sat down at the table, and prayed. Mueller took the staff in another room and prayed—not so much for God to "bless the food" but for Him to *provide* the food! Without fail, some supernatural intervention would occur. Frequently, a bakery truck would pull up to the receiving door full of day old bread and other baked goods to donate. They had not been called or notified in any way. It was simply God's perfect timing.

> *"But I know you can reach up and touch God when you pray. I've proved it to myself. It changed my life. And I want to convince other people."*
>
> **George Mueller**

One classic "snapshot" of faith came when George Mueller boarded a ship that was bound for Quebec. He had a ministry engagement there and could not afford to miss it or be late. Unfortunately, the fog was so dense, that the captain of the ship refused to launch. It would have been too dangerous.

In his journal, the captain wrote these words on that day: "We had George Mueller of Bristol on board. I had been on the bridge for twenty four hours and never left it, when George Mueller came to me and said, 'Captain, I have come to tell you I must be in Quebec on Saturday afternoon.' I told him it was impossible. 'Then very well, if your ship cannot take me, God will find some other way. I have never broken an engagement in fifty-seven years; let us go down to the chart room and pray.'

"I looked at that man of God and thought, 'What lunatic asylum can that man have come from, for I never heard of such a thing as this.' 'Mr. Mueller,' I said, 'do you know how dense the fog is?' He replied, 'No. My eye is not on the fog, but on the living God who controls every circumstance of my life.' He then knelt down and prayed one of the most simple prayers. When he had finished I was going to pray, but he put his hand on my shoulder and told me not to pray. 'As you do not believe He will answer, and as I believe He already has, there is no need for you to pray about it.'

"I looked at him, and Mueller said, 'Captain, I have known my Lord for fifty-seven years and there has never been a single day when I have failed to get an audience with the King. Get up, Captain, and open the door and you will find the fog has gone.' I got up—and the fog, indeed, was gone, and on that Saturday afternoon George Mueller kept his promise."

Mueller established very successful orphanages in England which were modeled throughout the world. For his unparalleled work in this area, Mueller is known as "The Father of Homeless Waifs (homeless children)."

So many Christians from the past have provided marvelous models of what it means to live by faith. Faith is not some sort of optional feature in the life of the disciple, it is essential. In fact, Hebrews 11:6 reminds us that it is impossible to please God without it.

If we are to take this passage literally, then George Mueller must have been most pleasing to our Father in Heaven.

Significant Contribution

He modeled the principle of living and ministering by faith through his orphanages and preaching ministry.

Recommended Reading

George Mueller, by Faith Coxe Bailey

APPLICATION

1. George Mueller struggled to trust God for the provisions necessary to open an orphanage until he meditated upon Psalm 81:10, "Open thy mouth wide and I will fill it." Can you name a facet of your life about which you feel uneasy and uncertain as to whether or not God is going to fill the need?

2. When Mueller was ten, he enrolled in the Cathedral Classic School to eventually become a clergyman. The goal was not to serve God, but to have an easy life. Is there any affluence that should be trimmed from a ministry of which you are a part?

3. Mueller never did public fundraising but asked only God to meet his financial needs. His goal was to show an unbelieving world the reality of a God who answers prayer. What visible need might you tell to no one but God?

4. Many days there were barely enough provisions to keep the ministry going. Mueller believed God wanted it that way, so he would be forced to pray often and depend upon God. One morning there was no food and things looked especially discouraging. Mueller decided that he and his staff would spend the day praying. By evening, all that was needed had come in—with some to spare. Get out your calendar and schedule a day of prayer.

   Date:

5. Mueller cared for 10,024 orphans. Name one fatherless child you could help.

   Name:

   What help will you offer?

JOURNAL RESPONSE

1. What did I learn from this historical mentor? (Character trait, truth, life principle or method?)

2. How do I feel about applying this to my life? (Challenged, frightened, liberated, stimulated?)

3. What next step should I take in response? (My personal application of this truth or principle.)

4. Who could encourage me and hold me accountable? (Friend, mentor, pastor, parent, etc.)

5. Why is this lesson important for me today? (How will this enable me to build God's Kingdom?)

DECLARATION 8:

It's my turn to invest my time, resources and money in God's Kingdom.

Eric Liddell

(1902-1945)

Eric Liddell had shocked the world. He was favored to win the 100 meter race in the 1924 Paris Olympics but refused to run on Sunday.

Eric was born to missionary parents in China. Early, he felt the call of God on his life to be a missionary. While being educated in Scotland, Eric gained national fame as a runner and rugby player, and was chosen to represent England at the Olympic games.

Four days later Eric Liddell won the 400 meter race in world record time! This was not his best event and most people thought a bronze medal would be quite an achievement for Eric. Winning the gold medal gave his native land of Scotland a new hero. Eric would prove to be as great a role model as he was athlete.

In the days following his Olympic victory, Eric was besieged with well wishers, reporters and fans. He took this new found fame and glory in stride. Humility and grace marked all of his public appearances. In one celebration following his graduation from college just one week after his Olympic triumph, Eric remembered the athletes whose homecomings were not so glorious with these words, "In the dust of defeat as well as in the laurels of victory there is glory to be found if one has done his best."

Behind the glamour and prestige of Olympic glory there was a deeper passion burning brightly within Eric Liddell. He knew the time had come to pursue the higher calling God had placed on his life.

Within weeks after returning from Paris, Eric chose a luncheon as the platform to announce his new direction. As usual, Eric was asked to give a speech. In it he highlighted the role of Tom McKerchar, his personal trainer, as one who made an important contribution to all of his athletic success. Sensing his sincerity the audience applauded Tom at the conclusion of Eric's speech. But Eric did not sit down as was expected following his speech. The smile on his face faded away; the audience sensed a seriousness about him. He explained that he had been offered and accepted a teaching position at the college in Tienstin, China and would be fully devoting himself to preparing for missionary life.

> *"In the dust of defeat as well as in the laurels of victory there is a glory to be found if one has done his best."*
>
> *Eric Liddell*

Here stood before them a young, intelligent world class athlete with more opportunities for fame, prosperity and success than most of them would ever know. But they should not have been surprised. Eric Liddell had shown the world he was a man of principle. Neither public opinion nor the lure of success could sway him from the call of God. He had made a decision to surrender his life, his talents and his future to the will of God.

Eric asked for and received a one year deferment on his teaching assignment in China. He would use this time to study theology at the Congregational College in Edinburgh. On weekends Eric traveled throughout Scotland and England holding evangelistic crusades. He knew God had given him a unique platform for influence and he was set on using it for God's glory. He spoke in theaters, churches, dance halls and social clubs; wherever an audience could be assembled, Eric was happy to share both his story and his Lord. Scores of people came to Christ in those 1924-25 crusades. Eric was not waiting until he arrived in China to serve as a laborer in the harvest fields of the Lord.

In the summer of 1925, the people of Scotland would have one last chance to see Eric run. Some 12,000 people crowded the event. Eric won all three of his races, the 100 meter, 200 meter and 400 meter events.

Finally the day had come for Eric to leave for China. The streets were lined with people cheering on their favorite son. A huge crowd gathered at the train station to see him off. In reverence and respect for his faith the crowd sang one of Eric's favorite hymns as the train pulled away from the station. At age 23, just one year after he had ridden the wave of public accolade out of the Paris Olympics, Eric Liddell was riding alone on a train across Europe headed for China.

He lived the rest of his life as a missionary in China, and died of a brain tumor while being held captive in a Japanese internment camp during WWII.

His life, documented in the film *Chariots of Fire*, is exemplified in the words of the apostle Paul. "Do you not know that in a race all the runners run, but only one gets the prize? Run in such a way as to get the prize. Everyone who competes in the games goes into strict training. They do it to get a crown that will not last; but we do it to get a crown that will last forever" (1Corinthians 9:24-25).

Significant Contribution

As an Olympic athlete, Eric Liddell showed the world that his eternal priorities were more important than temporal opportunities. He laid aside fame and fortune to pursue the call of God, serving among the unreached in China.

Recommended Reading

Eric Liddell, by Catherine Swift

APPLICATION

1. Eric Liddell refused to run in the Olympics on Sunday. What do you refuse to do on Sunday?

2. What is Exodus 20:9-11 about?

3. When Liddell refused to run on Sunday he was accused of being unpatriotic and legalistic. Was he?

4. Liddell wrote, "Ask yourself: If I know something to be true, am I prepared to follow it, even though it is contrary to what I want?. . .Will I follow it if it means being laughed at, if it means personal financial loss or some kind of hardship?" Will you? Tell God your answer in prayer.

5. Liddell wrote, "The bravest moment of a person's life is the moment when he looks at himself objectively without wincing, without complaining. However, self-examination that does not result in action is dangerous. What am I going to do about what I see? The action called for is surrender—of ourselves to God." During objective self-examination, what might you be inclined to wince or complain about?

6. Liddell demonstrated self-sacrificing compassion by rescuing wounded soldiers, whatever their nationality, at great risk to life and limb. In what ways are you demonstrating love for your "neighbor?"

7. Liddell died in a prison camp thousands of miles from his wife and children. Are you ready to die in service to God?

JOURNAL RESPONSE

1. What did I learn from this historical mentor? (Character trait, truth, life principle or method?)

2. How do I feel about applying this to my life? (Challenged, frightened, liberated, stimulated?)

3. What next step should I take in response? (My personal application of this truth or principle.)

4. Who could encourage me and hold me accountable? (Friend, mentor, pastor, parent, etc.)

5. Why is this lesson important for me today? (How will this enable me to build God's Kingdom?)

DECLARATION 9:

It's my turn to assume the role of a servant.

Florence Nightingale

(1820-1910)

Just like the rich young ruler in Luke 18, Florence Nightingale faced the choice of keeping her position in society, or following the plan of God for her life. This decision was a difficult one for Florence, being the well-educated, attractive and popular daughter of a prominent English banker. Florence felt sure God called her into His service when she was seventeen. However, it was not until she was twenty-two that she knew the direction for her life. It was then she was so moved by the plight of the sick and dying in England that she determined to help them no matter what the cost.

The nursing profession in the mid 1800's was not suitable for women of Florence's social status, she was told. Doctors informed the Nightingale family that most nurses were "drunkards, prostitutes, and given to immoral practices."

It was into the most respectable institution of nursing that Florence finally entered at the age of thirty-one. The decision made to follow God's call, despite what others might say, she eagerly learned all she could of nursing and hospital administration, excelling at both.

Several years later, Florence was asked to become the superintendent of nurses at Kings College Hospital. As she was making plans to accept the invitation, an item in the "Times" about the Crimean War caught her attention. "...no sufficient preparations have been made for the proper care of the wounded. Not only are there no dressers and nurses... Men (are) kept in some cases for a week without the hand of a medical man..." The article ended with the challenge, "Are there no devoted women amongst us able...to go forth to minister to the sick and suffering soldiers.... Are none...ready for such a work of mercy?" Florence's heart was stirred, and she responded immediately to the call.

At the request of the English government, Florence, became the organizer and administrator of a group of thirty-eight nurses who left within a week for the Crimean War. The conditions they found were horrible beyond description. The wounded were everywhere; in all available beds, on the floors and in the halls, many lying in their uniforms which were stiff with blood and covered with filth. Maggots crawled over them, eating the rotting flesh and finding their way into food supplies. Outside the sickroom window, in open view of the wounded, was a pile of amputated arms and legs.

> *"Oh, Lord, thou puttest into my heart this great desire to devote myself to the sick and sorrowful. I offer it to thee."*
>
> *Florence Nightingale*

Florence immediately went to work formulating a system to nurse the wounded, while devising plans that would secure mattresses, linens, bandages, soap, cleaning supplies, shirts, eating utensils, and proper ventilation for the hospital and the wounded. Often Florence would use her own funds or donations solicited from friends in England to purchase needed supplies. She equipped diet kitchens where more appropriate foods for the recovering could be made, and hired soldiers wives to operate a laundry in order to have clean clothes and linens for the hospital. Within weeks, amazing differences could be seen in the condition of the hospital, the morale and health of the wounded and the availability of supplies.

Florence, in the midst of all she was trying to reform, never neglected her job of nursing. She would spend hours in the wards looking after the wounded. Often she could be found at the bed of the most severe cases. She would encourage and comfort those deemed hopeless by the doctors, nursing them back to health, or saving a limb scheduled for amputation. The men came to idolize her. Late into the night, she would pass among the miles of beds, lamp in hand, making a final tour of the wards. It was from these nighttime rounds that she became known as "the lady with the lamp."

At the close of the war, Florence stayed on at the hospital for a few months to nurse the remaining soldiers until they, too, could return home. A British war ship was offered for her return, and England prepared for her arrival with brass bands and ceremonies. Florence had other plans and, using an assumed name, booked passage on a small steamer for the crossing to England. She traveled by train as an unknown passenger, walked from the train station and entered her home, unannounced through the back door.

Because of her development and promotion of a new nursing system and her monumental book, *Notes on Nursing,* Florence Nightingale has been called "the mother of the modern nursing profession."

Her life of service to others is summed up in her counsel to fellow workers. "Life is a splendid gift. There is nothing small in it, for the greatest things grow by God's law out of the smallest. But to live your life, you must discipline it. You must not fritter it away in fair purpose, erring act, inconstant will, but must make your thought, your work, your acts all work to the same end, and that end not in self but in God."

Significant Contribution

Florence Nightingale was among the first to balance the combination of humanitarian service with the preaching of the Gospel. Her innovative approach to nursing greatly influenced the future of the profession.

Recommended Reading

A Lost Commander, Florence Nightingale, by Mary Raymond Shipman Andrews

APPLICATION

1. A man fell deeply in love with Florence, and years later she described him as the "man I adored." They loved one another. He was rich and eligible, and she was clever and good-looking. They shared common interests. Why didn't they marry? Because of her conviction that God had called her to higher things. What kinds of things could be higher than marriage?

2. On July 1, 1850, Florence "lay in bed and called on God to save me." From what do people need to be saved?

3. With soldiers dying sometimes minutes after being treated, Florence said, "...I am weary of this hopeless work." Yet she wrote, "What I have done I shall continue doing." What does Galatians 6:9 say to you?

JOURNAL RESPONSE

1. What did I learn from this historical mentor? (Character trait, truth, life principle or method?)

2. How do I feel about applying this to my life? (Challenged, frightened, liberated, stimulated?)

3. What next step should I take in response? (My personal application of this truth or principle.)

4. Who could encourage me and hold me accountable? (Friend, mentor, pastor, parent, etc.)

5. Why is this lesson important for me today? (How will this enable me to build God's Kingdom?)

DECLARATION 10:

It's my turn to influence rather than be influenced.

William Carey

(1761-1834)

On August 1, 1786, at twenty-five years of age, William Carey was ordained as a minister. As the hands of the officiating ministers were laid on him, they had no way of knowing the full measure of what was stirring in William Carey's soul. His knowledge of geography and God-inspired vision for the world was like a spiritual geyser waiting to erupt.

William poured himself into local church ministry. But his dreams of reaching out to the far away lands never left him. He nurtured this passion for the world by reviewing the information collected on a home made globe. He reflected on the slighted or neglected countries of the world and praying that God would make a way for him to do something on behalf of the "heathen nations" living in darkness. His sister noted that she had never heard William pray without including the "heathen nations."

Carey's brilliant intellect and spiritual passion made him stand above other ministers with far more training and experience when it came to the needs of the world. Once while attending a ministers meeting, a question was posed about an island in the East Indies. No one knew anything about the place. After plenty of time had been given for others to respond, William Carey modestly rose to his feet and gave the location of the island and information he had gleaned about the spiritual condition of its inhabitants.

Once he was ordained, William Carey was invited to participate in the Ministers' Fraternal of the Northampton Association. It was at a meeting of this association in 1786 that William Carey was asked to pose a question that would form the basis of the group's discussion for the day. He proposed they consider "Whether the command given to the apostles to teach all nations was not binding on all succeeding ministers to the end of the world, seeing that the accompanying promise was of equal extent."

His suggestion was met with a harsh rebuke from the chairman, Mr. Ryland, who exclaimed, "Young man, sit down! You are an enthusiast. When God desires to converse with the heathen He'll do it without consulting you or me." Carey was publicly humiliated and received little if any support from his peers who saw his ideas as wildly imaginative.

"Expect great things from God. Attempt great things for God."

William Carey

The passion and genius William Carey possessed was well hidden beneath his rustic exterior. He was short, often poorly dressed, wore an ill fitted wig made of horse hair to cover his premature baldness and had hands cracked and stained from years of working with leather as a shoe maker. On the surface, Carey had more than enough reasons to abort the mission God had chiseled on his heart. But he did not give up.

Two years later, Carey met Thomas Potts, a young man who had been in America and seen first hand the evils of slave trade and the spiritual needs of the Indians. Potts implored William Carey to put his ideas in print. When Carey hedged on the idea Thomas Potts contributed ten pounds toward the printing of a pamphlet exhorting Christians to accept responsibility for the evangelization of the heathen.

Carey accepted the challenge and drew upon his eight years of research to write an eighty-seven page booklet entitled, *An*

Enquiry Into the Obligation of Christians to Use Means For the Conversion of the Heathen. In this booklet, Carey poured out his soul. He carefully documented the geographic, cultural and spiritual conditions of every known part of the world. From the early years of his childhood God had been preparing William Carey for this moment of destiny. Years of study, research and prayer were coming to a climax.

The influence of Carey's Booklet opened the door for Carey to speak at one of the associations' meetings in 1792. He preached from Isaiah 54:2-3, "Enlarge the place of thy tent...thy seed shall inhabit the Gentiles" (KJV). He summed up his fiery challenge to reach out to heathen nations with these words, "Expect great things from God. Attempt great things for God."

On October 2, 1792, a resolution was adopted creating the first Protestant mission agency and the first era of Protestant missions began.

Carey himself eventually went to India and was responsible for translating the Bible into eleven languages.

Significant Contributions

Because of his public stand for missions among pastors in England and his pioneer missionary efforts in India, William Carey is known as the Father of Modern Missions.

Recommended Reading

William Carey, by Basil Miller

APPLICATION

1. William Carey thanked God for the daily regularity with which his parents drilled him on scripture. "My mind was furnished with themes, which afterwards were often influential on my heart, when I had little leisure." Read Psalm 119, noting how often God's law, statutes, precepts, commands, and word are mentioned.

2. As a young man, Carey worked as a shoemaker. He made a map of the world on the wall over his cobbler's bench, so he could pray for each country while he worked. Before going to item #3, select several nations and pray for the advancement of the gospel there.

3. Carey wrote, "We must plan and plod as well as pray." What specific step will you take to participate in what you just prayed in #2 above? When will you take that step?

4. After seven years in India, Carey's first convert "became a Christian, not a European." What is a Christian? Can you find your definition in the Bible?

5. Carey said, "If what we attempt is a vision from God, we will receive His protection and provision. If the vision is our own making, we will experience privation and problems." What is a "great thing" you could attempt for God?

6. Late in life, Carey said to an admirer, "You have been speaking about Dr. Carey; when I am gone, say nothing about Dr. Carey - speak about Dr. Carey's Savior!" Write something about Dr. Carey's Savior.

JOURNAL RESPONSE

1. What did I learn from this historical mentor? (Character trait, truth, life principle or method?)

2. How do I feel about applying this to my life? (Challenged, frightened, liberated, stimulated?)

3. What next step should I take in response? (My personal application of this truth or principle.)

4. Who could encourage me and hold me accountable? (Friend, mentor, pastor, parent, etc.)

5. Why is this lesson important for me today? (How will this enable me to build God's Kingdom?)

DECLARATION 11:

It's my turn to love the unlovable.

William Booth

(1829-1912)

Before William Booth became a minister, he conducted services in small country places as a lay preacher. It was clear to everyone he had the poor in his heart and work, even as a teenager. When he got his local preacher's license in the Methodist church, his superintendent asked him to simply settle for a "regular" ministry as a minister in a church rather than the hard labor of working with the poor. Taking it even further, his doctor advised him against any kind of ministry, telling Booth that his health was so poor that he was totally unfit for the strain of the preacher's life. Booth humbly replied, "Unfit? Of course I am unfit in myself. But in the strength God gives me, I am going to do the thing God has called me to do."

That doctor had no way of knowing that Booth would eventually take on strenuous work among London's poor, physical labor that would make the life of a Methodist minister seem like a vacation. Nor did the doctor have any way of knowing that Booth would launch an organization of worldwide proportions and that he would live to be eighty three.

For over thirty years the Salvation Army and William Booth in particular were subject to some of the most vile persecution Christians suffered in modern times. But the "General" lived to see the day when his army would be honored around the world.

His own King Edward VII did so at Buckingham Palace in 1904. When the king asked him to sign his autograph album, Booth summed up his life's work as he wrote:

Your Majesty,
Some men's ambition is art,
Some men's ambition is fame,
Some men's ambition is gold,
My ambition is the souls of men.

His wife shared this same ambition for lost souls, and especially for the poor. Once, as a young girl she saw a convict being taken by the constable and an angry mob to the lockup. In all the yelling, it seemed to her that this poor man didn't have a friend in the world, and his utter loneliness struck her. Quick as the thought, she sprang to his side and marched down the street with him, determined that he should know that there was one soul that felt for him. Such was the compassion that both of the Booths felt for the poor and downcast.

A contrast between two lives was noted by Dr. Harold Luccock. The first was a woman who died in London, famous as "the best dressed woman in Europe." She left almost a thousand frocks, but with each frock she had worn "the same unseeing eyes, the same deaf ears, the same enameled, painted face." The second was a man who died in the same city, with but one suit, blue with a red collar on the coat. He was William Booth, founder of the Salvation Army. He had but one costume, but he lived a thousand lives. When J. Wilbur Chapman was in London, he had the opportunity to meet Booth, then past eighty years old. After listening to stories of his trials, conflicts and victories, the American evangelist asked the general if he would disclose his secret for success. "He hesitated for a second," Chapman said, "and I saw tears come

> **"I want a life spent in putting other people right."**
>
> **William Booth**

into his eyes and steal down his cheeks, and then he said, 'I will tell you the secret. God has had all there was of me. There have been men with greater brains than I, men with greater opportunities; but from the day I got the poor of London on my heart, and a vision of what Jesus Christ could do with the poor of London, I made up my mind that God would have all of William Booth there was.'" Dr. Chapman said he went away from the meeting knowing "that the greatness of a man's power is the measure of his surrender."

Just before his death, Booth appeared a final time to speak. His health was failing, and he had only one eye. To an audience of over 4,000 he spoke for an hour and a half. "I want to do more for humanity," he said, "and I want to do a great deal more for Jesus. There are thousands of poor, wretched, suffering and sinning people crying out to us for help, and I want to do something for them!" The poor and the entire world have never been the same since Booth and the Salvation Army have been here.

Significant Contribution

William Booth began a movement that changed the way his nation viewed and addressed the poor. Because of his relentless efforts in helping all poverty stricken people, the Salvation Army now has branches worldwide. It is still touching lives today with generosity and compassion, offering hope and teaching the gospel. The Salvation Army has affected innumerable lives for Christ as a result of Booth's vision.

Recommended Reading

William Booth, Founder of the Salvation Army, by Harold Begbie

APPLICATION

1. As an apprentice pawnbroker, William Booth observed the poor pledging their treasures (rings, watches, etc.) in return for a loan at interest. If all wealth is gained by exchanging one thing for another, what are the characteristics of true treasure?

2. Seeking assurance of salvation, Booth's wife, Catherine, read the words to Charles Wesley's hymn:

    My God, I am thine; what a comfort divine:
    What a blessing to know that Jesus is mine!

    What does it mean to "belong to God"?

3. Hundreds of young people, as officers in the army Booth founded, promised, "For Christ's sake, to feed the poor, clothe the naked, love the unlovable, and befriend the friendless." What have you done lately to accomplish each of those four objectives?

4.   Booth brought the gospel message to the streets with innovative open air meetings. How are you moving beyond the four walls of the church to share Christ with others?

JOURNAL RESPONSE

1. What did I learn from this historical mentor? (Character trait, truth, life principle or method?)

2. How do I feel about applying this to my life? (Challenged, frightened, liberated, stimulated?)

3. What next step should I take in response? (My personal application of this truth or principle.)

4. Who could encourage me and hold me accountable? (Friend, mentor, pastor, parent, etc.)

5. Why is this lesson important for me today? (How will this enable me to build God's Kingdom?)

DECLARATION 12:

It's my turn to bless the nations.

David Livingstone

(1813-1873)

As a new Christian, seventeen year old David Livingstone had no desire to go to the mission field. However, the Lord had a plan for his life, and because Livingstone was faithful, he is now considered to be one of the greatest missionaries ever.

David Livingstone determined he was going to value what God valued—and his burden for unreached peoples mushroomed. He had planned to be a missionary and serve in Asia, but God had other plans. It didn't matter much to him, as long as he could bless some unreached nation. As it turned out, Dr. Livingstone was the first white man to share Christ on the continent of Africa. This is the kind of pioneer spirit that God can use in the most needy of places.

Trail-blazing is never easy. Livingstone wrestled with gaining enough support from those who knew of his endeavor back home. Due to his poor physical condition, he brought a goat with him, because his doctors had instructed that he drink goat's milk on a regular basis. He later surrendered that goat to a tribal chief, in order to make a covenant with that village. This turned out to be a major breakthrough. His willingness to surrender all that he had to complete the task of reaching this tribe, opened up all kinds of doors of opportunity for gaining favor with other tribes. Soon, great inroads were made for this white man on a dark continent.

He was one of the first to practice the method of sharing the gospel with the natives in the structure of their own culture. This led to a much more effective means of evangelizing other people groups throughout the world.

Along with this notoriety, Livingstone is also known as one of the greatest explorers of all time. Livingstone "opened" Africa, a previously mysterious and unexplored continent, for the evangelization of the natives and the development of commerce with the rest of the world.

> *"Whatever way my life may be spent as best to promote the glory of our gracious God, I feel anxious to do it. . ."*
>
> *David Livingstone*

Through his missionary career, Livingstone developed a deep love for those he evangelized. This love, coupled with his writing talents, allowed Livingstone to be largely influential in ridding Europe of one of its greatest evils—slavery.

On one afternoon, Dr. Livingstone received a letter from his homeland. The note read: "We are happy to hear of your success there in Africa. We are ready to join you, if you can tell us of any good roads." This angered Livingstone. These were the same people who had refused to endorse what he had done in his pioneer work, earlier. His response was simple but telling and profound. He simply wrote: "I do not need people who will come if there are good roads. I need those who will come if there are no roads at all."

That was David Livingstone! He was a spiritual entrepreneur in the area where God needed one most. Although the work of converting the nationals was slow, he continued inland with the message of God's love for all the world. His only real convert was a journalist named Stanley, who pursued him there, not knowing if Livingstone had been killed or tortured by the tribes he had met. Livingstone finally died after years of pioneer work in the land he had come to embrace as his own. When his body was discovered, it surprised no one that he was found on his knees, praying. He had been praying for a spiritual harvest he'd not yet seen on that continent—but one that would come later as a result of his work.

Significant Contribution

David Livingstone's pioneer spirit "unlocked" the continent of Africa and paved the way for future laborers to bring the Gospel to the unreached peoples of that Continent's interior.

Recommended Reading

Livingstone the Pathfinder, by Basil Matthews

APPLICATION

1. In human terms, David Livingstone's life was filled with disillusion: he failed as a husband; he failed as a father; he failed as a missionary; he had failed as a geographer and as a liberator. This raises a couple questions:

   A. Is the worth of a life judged by immediate or long term consequences?

   B. Is the worth of a life judged by its successes in results and consequences, or by the motives and integrity of the agent?

   How do you defend your answers to these questions?

2. In your own words, what would you say is the meaning and purpose of our temporary existence here, in a world where much is doubtful, obscure and incomprehensible?

3. Livingstone said, "Men may think I covet fame, but I make it a rule never to read aught (anything) written in my praise." What does Proverbs 27:21 say to you?

4. Livingstone said, "If the good Lord gives me favor and permits me to finish my work, I shall thank and bless Him, though it has cost me untold toil, pain, and travail; this trip has made my hair all grey." What should be our response if the Lord does not permit us to finish "our" work?

JOURNAL RESPONSE

1. What did I learn from this historical mentor? (Character trait, truth, life principle or method?)

2. How do I feel about applying this to my life? (Challenged, frightened, liberated, stimulated?)

3. What next step should I take in response? (My personal application of this truth or principle.)

4. Who could encourage me and hold me accountable? (Friend, mentor, pastor, parent, etc.)

5. Why is this lesson important for me today? (How will this enable me to build God's Kingdom?)

DECLARATION 13:

It's my turn to become a threat to the kingdom of darkness.

John Paton

(1824-1907)

In the late 1800's, when John Paton arrived in The New Hebrides Islands located northeast of Australia, he found a barbaric, cannibalistic people who practiced sorcery and witchcraft.

He felt the call of God early in his life to become a missionary in the Pacific Islands. He began his mission career while a college student in Glasgow, Scotland, ministering among the poor of the city. Financial difficulties plagued young Paton, and several times he left school in order to raise money that he might return the next semester. It was these odd jobs that taught Paton many of the skills and fortitude he would couple with the Gospel to win the natives of New Hebrides Islands to Christ.

Having purchased land from the natives on the island of Tanna, Paton began the daunting task of establishing a missionary work among them. He was not the first to attempt to bring the Gospel to Tanna. Several had preceded him and had been killed or run off the island - a history the natives were quite proud of!

In the first few months after arriving, Paton's wife and infant son died of malaria. Paton himself was afflicted with malaria at least fourteen times in his first few years on New Hebrides.

The people's initial curiosity quickly gave way to hatred and fear as John began to teach against their beliefs and proclaim

Jehovah as the only true God. Often as he worked he would be surrounded by musket or hatchet toting natives intent on killing him.

As Paton taught the people, he was violently opposed by three Sacred Men. They claimed to control life and death, sickness and rain through dances, rituals and sacrifices to their god, Nahak. An important part of their craft was accomplished by securing a piece of fruit or other food which an individual had eaten.

One Sunday the Sacred Men claimed to be able to kill Paton, and he determined to put them to the test. Giving each of them a piece of fruit of which he had eaten, he challenged them to kill him by the powers of Nahak and with out the help of muskets, arrows or other weapons. The Sacred Men immediately wrapped the fruit in the leaves of a sacred tree and rolled this into the shape of a candle. Lighting a fire, they began to slowly burn the candles. During all of this they chanted incantations and danced, waving the candles wildly. By this time, all the natives had fled in terror, but Paton stayed so the Sacred Men could see the lack of effect they were having upon him. When they had exhausted themselves without harm to Paton, they determined to gather all the Sacred Men of the island together and promised that Paton would be dead within a week.

> *"...we have all in our Lord Jesus for peace and joy in all circumstances."*
>
> **John Paton**

All week Paton continued to pray against the Sacred Men and their power, so that the people might see that Jehovah was protecting him. Men continually came throughout the week to inquire of his health, and returned to the Sacred Men disappointed. On Sunday, Paton returned to the village in perfect health. The Sacred Men admitted to the people that they had indeed tried to kill Paton by the powers of Nahak, but that Paton's God was stronger and had protected him. This crucial test proved to them the power of Jehovah.

The natives were a fearful people, however, and were often swayed by the speeches of their Chiefs and Sacred Men who wished to harm Paton. So after four years on the island of Tanna, he was finally forced to flee. Later, however, while Paton was living on a nearby island, the people begged him to return and teach them.

The people of Tanna finally did embrace the Gospel. Confidence in God and the power of prayer allowed Paton, and later others, to overcome the dark forces at work on Tanna and win the spiritual battle that was being waged.

Significant Contribution

John Paton reminds us that it is right to endure hardship, suffer and risk death in the process of obedience to God's call.

Recommended Reading

John G. Paton, Hero of the South Seas, by Bessie G. Byrum

APPLICATION

1. In his later years, John Paton influenced young people to go into missionary endeavors. Name a handful of individuals younger than you whom you could influence.

2. Paton worked in the midst of cannibals. Further, these "savages" were from time to time stirred up by mistreatment including rape and murder at the hands of crews of vessels in the region. Paton stayed. At what point is the safety of the missionary to be an overriding consideration, and when should safety be cast into the lap of God?

3. Paton was engaged in "spiritual warfare." What principles does Ephesians 6:10-20 provide in confronting evil?

4. Paton returned to western "civilized" countries to stir interest in missionary enterprises as well as arouse sentiment against the liquor trade, traffic in girls, and other "crimes wherein man so far outdoes the barbarian and descends below the beast." He saw such distractions as impediments to missionary fruitfulness. What connection do you see?

5. Paton was a missionary to the city of Glasgow for ten years. Is there a city you are called to penetrate with the claims and identity of Jesus?

JOURNAL RESPONSE

1. What did I learn from this historical mentor? (Character trait, truth, life principle or method?)

2. How do I feel about applying this to my life? (Challenged, frightened, liberated, stimulated?)

3. What next step should I take in response? (My personal application of this truth or principle.)

4. Who could encourage me and hold me accountable? (Friend, mentor, pastor, parent, etc.)

5. Why is this lesson important for me today? (How will this enable me to build God's Kingdom?)

DECLARATION 14:

It's my turn to reproduce other laborers.

Dawson Trotman

(1906-1956)

A young sailor approached Dawson Trotman, on board a ship one day, and asked him to help him grow. "Daws", as his friends affectionately called him, clarified that what the sailor was really asking for was to be discipled. He then agreed to help the young sailor over the next several months. During the experience, this sailor's life was so dramatically changed, that he brought a buddy of his to Daws and asked if Daws would disciple him, as well. The reply startled both sailors: "Absolutely not." Then, Daws went on to say, "If your friend is going to be discipled, it will have to be you who does it."

So, the two of them connected in a discipleship relationship. Upon their completion, the chain continued. Both went out and found someone whom they could invest their lives. This happened again and again and again. Once a man was discipled, he was expected to go and disciple someone else.

What makes this story so intriguing is that it literally transformed the atmosphere on the ship. Eventually, the FBI was called to investigate what was going on. People thought some sort of cult had emerged. Others wondered about the odd behavior of what was once a "normal" group of sailors. Clearly, things were different. What's more, once the FBI began to investigate, it took them six months to sift through all the men who had been discipled in order to find Daws—the one who had started the whole thing!

This is how the number of Jesus' disciples multiplied in the New Testament days. Early Christians took responsibility to "mentor" one another, one by one. For nearly three centuries the early church continued in the mandate to reproduce themselves; it was each one, reach one. It had not yet entered their minds to sit back and let the "clergy" do all the work. Every one was a minister.

But how might this look if it were to happen today? Could a movement like the one that began in the first and second centuries occur in the twentieth century? Our contemporary world had not yet seen what wide spread, spiritual reproduction might look like in modern times, when Dawson Trotman began his ministry. Folks had become familiar with "mass evangelism", but not with large scale discipleship, and exponential growth. Yet deep in Trotman's heart-he knew it was not only possible, but it was imperative. It was against this backdrop, that Dawson Trotman, initiated his disciplemaking movement known as the Navigators.

> *"God can do more through one man who is 100 percent dedicated to him than through 100 men who are only 90 percent dedicated."*
>
> *Dawson Trotman*

That same kind of network of training and reproducing people ought to exist in every established local church in our country. We must remember, however, that spiritual multiplication through reproduction happens one life at a time. Babies are generally not born in mass—neither are disciples of Jesus Christ. Dawson Trotman proved to us (as did our Lord) that mentoring disciples is slow and painstaking—but if done well, is the only way our world is going to be effectively reached.

Significant Contribution

Dawson Trotman reintroduced the church to the lost priority of disciplemaking and spiritual reproduction. The Navigators are continuing to multiply disciples throughout the world.

Recommended Reading

DAWS: The Story of Dawson Trotman, Founder of the Navigators, by Betty Lee Skinner

APPLICATION

1. Twice, Dawson Trotman enrolled in Christian colleges, only to withdraw because of the urgency he felt for continuing his ministry. How should a person decide whether he should "go back to school" or use some other means of "getting an education?"

2. Trotman believed that a discipling relationship culminates in the new believer bringing someone else to faith in Christ. According to that standard, have you been discipled? Have you discipled anyone?

3. Scripture memorization was strongly emphasized in Trotman's life and ministry. How important do you think it is to memorize Scripture?

    How important, according to the Bible, is Scripture memorization?

4. Select a verse you have never memorized and do so now. In the space below, write it from memory.

5. Trotman drowned while rescuing a young girl who had fallen from a boat. In an obituary, *Time* magazine described him as "always holding someone up." Make a guess: how would *Time* magazine describe you in an obituary?

JOURNAL RESPONSE

1.   What did I learn from this historical mentor? (Character trait, truth, life principle or method?)

2.   How do I feel about applying this to my life? (Challenged, frightened, liberated, stimulated?)

3.   What next step should I take in response? (My personal application of this truth or principle.)

4.   Who could encourage me and hold me accountable? (Friend, mentor, pastor, parent, etc.)

5.   Why is this lesson important for me today? (How will this enable me to build God's Kingdom?)

DECLARATION 15:

It's my turn to surrender my life to God's will for me.

Hudson Taylor

(1832-1905)

Twelve-year-old Hudson Taylor sat with his siblings enthralled as his father expounded on one of his favorite topics: China. It was a land of mystery and intrigue known for silk, jade and tea. It was also a land in great need and potential for harvest.

"Why are there only a half dozen Protestants working in that great land?" mused James Taylor. Young Hudson chimed in, "When I am a man I mean to be a missionary and go to China!" The thought was amusing for the Taylor family as they got up from the table. Sickly little Hudson surviving the rigorous life of a missionary to China? It seemed like an impossibility.

In the summer of 1849, Hudson Taylor was all alone with a tract that pierced his heart with the truth of the gospel. His mother had been praying for him at the time of his conversion. She knew before he told her that the burden of sin had been rolled away.

By the end of the year Hudson had encountered his first season of spiritual battle. By December of 1849 he became obsessed with the fear of his potential for apostasy. He was keenly aware of God's presence but something was not right. He had an intense realization of his propensity for failure and feelings of unworthiness overwhelmed him. To young Hudson this was a life and death matter. Everything was at stake. He must settle the issues, whatever they may be, that kept him from total abandonment to God's will for his life.

All alone, just as it had been when he was converted, Hudson fell to his knees in prayer. He cried out to God asking for grace to keep him true, to break the power of sin and made a fresh dedication of himself to God. He promised to go anywhere and do anything, surrendering his life to God's will.

In that moment, God met Hudson Taylor with a deeply rooted conviction that his prayers had been answered. And with what seemed to be as clear as an audible voice, God spoke, "Then go for me to China." From that moment, his mind was made up. Nothing could deter him from pursuing the call of God that had been so clearly given.

> *"Our aim is not elaborate appeals for help, but rather to obtain successful laborers. First in earnest prayer to God to thrust forth laborers and second the deepening of the spiritual life of the church, so that men should be unable to stay at home."*
>
> **Hudson Taylor**

But what does a seventeen year old boy do to prepare for missionary service in China? Just finding a book about China would be a challenge. Hudson Taylor inquired of Mr. Whitworth, the founder and superintendent of the Sunday school. From Mr. Whitworth, Hudson obtained a copy of the writings of Luke in the Mandarin dialect. With this he diligently launched his study of the Chinese language. Within weeks his hard work and ingenuity had enabled him to decipher 500 Chinese words!

Hudson soon realized that he did not have to wait for the time he could actually go to be involved in ministry to China. He could pray and encourage others to pray. He could give in support of others who were ready to go. But in his heart Hudson was deeply burdened for the millions of Chinese living beyond the port cities of China who had no way of hearing the Good News. He had to go and tell them.

Hudson learned of a book written about China from a Christian perspective. The Congregational minister in his town was said to have a copy. In early 1850 he went to borrow it, hoping to deepen his understanding of how to prepare for service in China. "Why do you want to read it?" asked the minister as he pulled Barnsley's book from the shelf. Hudson explained his desire to go to China as a missionary. "And how do you propose to get there?" It was a question Hudson had not thought about in detail. He mumbled something about the disciples going out without means at the Lord's command.

"Ah, my boy, as you grow older you will get wiser than that. Such an idea would do very well in the days when Christ himself was on earth, but not now."

Hudson read the book anyway. His resolve continued to deepen. In a letter to his sister Amelia he wrote, "Poor, neglected China! Scarcely anyone cares about it. And that immense country, containing nearly a fourth of the human race, is left in ignorance and darkness." He put aside his feather bed as a means of preparing himself for the rigors of life in the interior of China and redoubled his efforts to learn Chinese.

Three years later, on September 19, 1853, at just over twenty-one years of age, Hudson Taylor was the only passenger on the freight ship Dumfries sailing for China. It was a voyage that lasted twenty-three weeks from Liverpool to Shanghai. It was a journey of faith that would last a life time. Hudson Taylor had surrendered his life to the will and call of God. That calling was to China. Not just a land but a people who were waiting for the gospel.

With that child-like faith, he poured out his life in China, enduring persecution, poverty and many physical ailments. He asked only God for financial support, and through his tireless efforts and constant prayers, he began the China Inland Mission. His passion for the lost and his complete faith in Christ have seldom been equaled.

Significant Contribution

Hudson Taylor initiated a new era of missionary activity by moving beyond the coast lands and focusing on the untapped interior of China.

Recommended Reading

Hudson Taylor, by Hudson Taylor

APPLICATION

1.   Hudson Taylor's parents dedicated him to God and educated him at home where they introduced him to the writings of great men. James Taylor took the matter of his children's training very seriously, spending a great deal of time with them, and often taking them into his prayer closet to witness firsthand God's faithfulness. When is the next time you will pray with children?

2.   James Taylor prayed specifically that God would give him a son that would devote his life to China. His prayers were answered when five-year-old Hudson announced, "When I am a man I will be a missionary in China." In the Bible, God often answered prayers for deliverance by sending a son (Moses, Jesus, and others). Pray for unborn children.

3. Upon dissecting a contaminated body with other lab students, Taylor accidentally pricked his finger. The supervisor told him to go home as fast as he could and put his affairs in order, saying, "You are a dead man." But God healed him through a slow recovery. Write a prayer thanking God for times when he snatched you from death (car accident, illness, etc.) with the confidence that He is not finished with you yet.

4. Taylor wrote, "Nor is God's work ever intended to be stationary, but always advancing." Has your part of the world been penetrated with the claims and identity of Christ? Write your next step in doing so.

JOURNAL RESPONSE

1. What did I learn from this historical mentor? (Character trait, truth, life principle or method?)

2. How do I feel about applying this to my life? (Challenged, frightened, liberated, stimulated?)

3. What next step should I take in response? (My personal application of this truth or principle.)

4. Who could encourage me and hold me accountable? (Friend, mentor, pastor, parent, etc.)

5. Why is this lesson important for me today? (How will this enable me to build God's Kingdom?)

Passing on the Baton as a Laborer

A group of police recruits were in class ready to take their final examination. They were asked by their instructor how they would respond to the following city-wide disaster:

> A young boy is drowning in a nearby lake. A woman's purse has been stolen on a main street downtown. A car has just struck a fire hydrant and water is spraying out of control. If that wasn't enough, an attempted bank robbery has turned into a hostage crisis.

One by one the recruits were called upon to stand to their feet and verbalize a plan of action. Finally, at the back of the room, one recruit dared to be honest, saying, "Remove uniform; mingle with crowd."

As we look around us or even watch the evening news, we are tempted to respond similarly. The path of least resistance in the face of desperate need is to remove the fish lapel pin from our coat or the cross from around our neck and blend with the crowd. If Jesus were walking the earth today, looking at the masses of our generation, He'd likely draw the same conclusion that He did 2000 years ago in Matthew 9:37-38: "The harvest is plentiful but the laborers are few. Ask the Lord of the harvest, therefore to send out laborers into his harvest field."

Isn't it interesting that when Jesus gazed at the masses, a microcosm of the world's population, He drew one conclusion. Not six or eight complex steps toward a solution, but one simple conclusion about what those people needed. It was laborers. What an intriguing word. What a compelling term to encompass all that was necessary to meet the needs of the people. Laborers.

He told his disciples, whom he had already converted from laymen to laborers, to pray that God would "send" more laborers into the vast harvest of human need. The word "send" was a passionate Aramaic word. It is the same word used in scripture to describe how Jesus "cast" out wicked spirits from a demonized person. It literally means "to thrust or to boot out." Jesus was commanding us to pray that God would "boot out" laborers into the huge harvest field!

To underscore how crucial this issue is to Jesus, be reminded that He issued very few prayer requests during His ministry. He prayed often—but only issued a handful of requests for prayer. This was one of the few: Pray that the Lord of the harvest would send out laborers! He apparently took this seriously. What do you think?

In fact, the primary purpose in Jesus' selection of His twelve disciples centered around this very issue. His objective wasn't to help them feel closer to God, or experience "goosebumps" from watching Him heal blind men. It was to turn laypeople into laborers. Do you remember what He said when He recruited them? "Follow me, and I will make you fishers of men" (Matthew 4:19). The call came with the conversion.

If this is not motivation enough for us, consider this principle: the natural result of maturity should be that a person begins to work. Labor and responsibility come with adulthood. Suppose you were the parent of a thirty-five year old son. Describing him to a friend one day, you say, "You know, I love my son. But, there is one small quirk about his lifestyle I find difficult to deal with. He, uh...he doesn't work. He's never held down a job in his life. Oh, he tried working once. It lasted two days. Then, he was back home on the sofa watching TV all day. I'm really not sure if he'll ever change."

Doesn't that scenario sound a bit odd and unhealthy? Then why isn't it equally odd and unhealthy for us to have been in the church for years and years-yet we've never really done anything? So often we never become spiritual laborers.

So, just what is a "laborer?" If you check the dictionary, you'll find this definition.

> ***Labor:*** *Toil or tribute offered for a cause; it can make weary, but also produces fruit.*

What a concise yet candid summary. In this case, the cause is the advancement of God's rule and reign on earth. "Thy kingdom come" was the objective of Jesus' labor.

This labor can take on many forms. It may be done in your church. It may be behind-the-scenes service offered in a soup kitchen downtown. It may be investing in one person over an extended period of time. It could be teaching a Bible study, sharing Christ on the streets, or washing the frail, wrinkled body of an elderly person in a retirement home. And it might just be moving to a cross-cultural setting and ministering to an unreached people group.

We believe, however, there are some common characteristics shared by all effective laborers. We are convinced that all fruitful laborers:

1) Are intimate disciples of Jesus Christ.
2) Use their gifts to advance God's kingdom.
3) Reproduce other laborers in their ministry.

None of these characteristics require that you be in full-time, vocational ministry. Some laborers, of course, will be; but it is crucial for most to stay in the marketplace at their jobs functioning as a fully devoted "laborer" for Christ. In other words, it is a paradigm shift where a man is transformed from being a plumber who happens to be a Christian, to being a Christian who happens to be a plumber. This is the transformation Jesus wants to make in every one of our lives.

It is remarkable to consider that if we all would commit to becoming "laborers" where we live and to obeying His personal instruction to us, the task of the Great Commission could be fulfilled. Remember, this was Jesus' solution to the state of the multitudes: *Laborers.* Stop and evaluate your life in light of this definition of a laborer. How are you doing? Are you using your gifts in a strategic way? Can you point to how God's kingdom is advancing because of your labor? Are you reproducing spiritually?

No matter where you are in your spiritual journey, you can become a productive Kingdom worker or laborer. Sometime you will need to take a first step demonstrating your commitment to move beyond sitting in the pew to serving in the fields. Your commitment may be an emotional "crisis moment" where you determine before God to cultivate intimate communion with Him, use your gifts in active service and reproduce other laborers. But not all commitments are emotional. You may quietly and sincerely make a matter of fact decision before God to become a laborer. Whatever the circumstances, God knows your heart and that is what counts.

On the next few pages we have expanded on the fifteen characteristics of world-changing Christians. *The Laborer's Declaration* outlines the values and priorities of a Kingdom worker in fifteen affirmation statements. We believe these words will solidify the thoughts and feelings many potential laborers have developed as a result of studying the lives of historical mentors presented in this book. As you read the affirmation statements of *The Laborer's Declaration*, ask God to show you what He wants you to do in response.

The Laborer's Declaration

Like a runner in the relay race of human history, I accept the baton of responsibility to reach my generation for Christ. I cannot live for today thinking only of myself. I cannot pretend the unreached are not lost, hell is not real, and I am not accountable for the needs around me.

Laborers from other generations have gone before me. They have taken their turn at using their gifts to build God's Kingdom. Today, I commit myself to join their ranks, as a laborer in my generation. It's my turn.

1. I affirm that being a laborer will require a *complete surrender* to the Lordship of Christ. **It's my turn to die to self.**

2. I affirm the need for *intimacy with God* as the foundation for service. **It's my turn to embrace God through worship.**

3. I affirm the *priority of prayer* as the driving force behind all Kingdom advancement. **It's my turn to intercede for the lost.**

4. I affirm the importance of *pursuing obedience* with reckless abandon. **It's my turn to sacrifice for the cause of Christ.**

5. I affirm that *only through Jesus* can we have relationship with God and hope for eternity. **It's my turn to share the Gospel.**

6. I affirm the Word of God is my *final authority* in all of life. **It's my turn to stand for what is true and right.**

7. I affirm *God has designed a lifestyle* for me that demands supernatural power. **It's my turn to live by faith.**

8. I affirm that *I am accountable* for everything God has given me. **It's my turn to invest my time, resources and money in God's Kingdom.**

9. I affirm that *we gain our lives* only when we *give them away.* **It's my turn to assume the role of a servant.**

10. I affirm the *need to be different* when the values of my culture contradict the values of the Kingdom. **It's my turn to influence rather than be influenced.**

11. I affirm the character of God is expressed to the world through *unconditional love.* **It's my turn to love the unlovable.**

12. I affirm *God's purpose* to establish His church from all the peoples of the earth. **It's my turn to bless the nations.**

13. I affirm I am *entering into conflict,* facing the reality of spiritual warfare. **It's my turn to become a threat to the kingdom of darkness.**

14. I affirm the *strategy of Jesus* for world conquest is spiritual multiplication. **It's my turn to reproduce other laborers.**

15. I affirm that I must respond *with urgency* to the window of opportunity that God has opened for me. **It's my turn to surrender my life to God's calling and will for me.**

Signature _____

Date _____

A Final Word of Caution . . .

It is our prayer that you have progressed through the material presented in this book and wholeheartedly embraced *The Laborer's Declaration*. Living out the *It's My Turn* affirmation statements in that declaration will prove to be a challenge. Every "crisis" experience must be followed by a growth process if it is to bear fruit over the long haul. We would like to leave you with a few practical suggestions to help you take your place in the relay race of human history, taking your turn to change the world.

1. Expect opposition from the enemy.

Your decision to "go all out" for God has not gone unnoticed by the forces of darkness. When soldiers get closer to the front lines of a battle, the fighting gets more intense. But, you have nothing to fear; "the One who is in you is greater than the one who is in the world" (1 John 4:4). But it would be naive to ignore the reality of spiritual conflict. Satan would love to make you a casualty of this spiritual war.

Remember to put on the full armor of God each day. Appropriate the preserving grace of God by His Spirit. He who has begun a good work in you will be faithful to complete it!

2. Beware of the Elijah Syndrome.

Following the great victory on Mount Carmel against the prophets of Baal, Elijah hit rock bottom. He panicked upon hearing the threats of Jezebel and ran for his life. All alone at Mount Horeb, Elijah poured out his soul before God, "I have been very zealous for the LORD God Almighty. The Israelites have rejected your covenant, broken down your altars, and put our prophets to death with the sword. I am the only one left, and now they are trying to kill me too" (1 Kings 19:10).

Elijah was convinced that he was the only one who was faithful to Jehovah. Upon facing opposition from the enemy, he bought into a lie that Satan has used successfully over and over again. You too will be tempted to look around your church or campus and believe you are the only faithful remaining "prophet of God." But listen to God's perspective on Elijah's situation, "I reserve seven thousand in Israel—whose knees have not bowed down to Baal and whose mouths have not kissed him" (1 Kings 19:18).

In spite of how it may appear you are not alone either. God always has a remnant. Ask God to open your eyes to the like-minded laborers in your area. Encourage one another as you work together to build God's Kingdom.

3. Deal with rejection graciously.

Some people will not understand the commitments you have made in *The Laborer's Declaration*. Laborers from every generation have been branded as radicals, mavericks and fanatics. Even members of your family, church, or campus group may find it difficult to accept your new found zeal in pursuing God's agenda for your life.

The apostle Paul gives laborers of every generation some very important words of instruction on this subject. In 2 Corinthians 6, Paul lists many of the hardships he faced in the process of obedience. This included dishonor, bad reports and being regarded as an impostor—all of this on top of imprisonment, beatings and sleepless nights! But in this same passage Paul emphasized the importance of "purity, understanding, patience...kindness and sincere love" (2 Corinthians 6:6). As you face rejection and misunderstanding, ask God to empower you with the fruit of the Holy Spirit.

4. *Guard your heart against pride.*

Making a sincere commitment to be a laborer will open the door of blessing on your life. Expect God to use you to advance His Kingdom. As you begin to experience results, you will be tempted to glory in what you have accomplished. Beware. God does not share His glory with anyone. One of the most common exit ramps from fruitful Kingdom service is pride. Remember the admonition of Peter who said, "God opposes the proud but gives grace to the humble. Humble yourselves therefore, under God's mighty hand, that he may lift you up in due time" (1 Peter 5:5-6).

5. *Balance your zeal with wisdom.*

Paul admonished the church in Rome saying, "Never be lacking in zeal, but keep your spiritual fervor, serving the Lord" (Romans 12:11). The church in North America is in desperate need of zealous laborers. But Solomon helps us maintain perspective with these words, "It is not good to have zeal without knowledge, nor to be hasty and miss the way" (Proverbs 19:2).

Seek out godly counsel and mature co-workers. Cooperate with existing ministry structures whenever possible. Season your words with love. Beware of alienating those around you by plowing ahead without first counting the cost.

6. *Work to keep your vision fresh.*

One of the most common statements your skeptics will make is that your new found vision will never last. "It's a new fad." "Youthful zeal." "Wait and see." It is true; feelings come and go.

But being a laborer is not about riding an emotional tidal wave into heaven. Reality checks will come all too often.

Like thousands of others who have gone before us, you *can* persevere in your commitment to live a life of total abandonment to the cause of Christ. By God's grace you *can* stand against the force of a hostile culture that seeks to water down your vision. At one time or another you will ask yourself, "What's the use?" In all likelihood, a moment of weakness will overtake you and you will fail. Perhaps miserably. Don't give up! Appropriate the forgiving grace of God and get back into the battle. Draw upon the power of accountability relationships, keeping in mind the admonition of the writer of Hebrews who said, "let us consider how we may spur one another on toward love and good deeds... all the more as you see the Day approaching" (Hebrews 10:24-25).

How to Benefit from Biographies

Historical role models provide us with a source of passive mentoring from which all Christians may benefit. Regardless of our circumstances, we can surround ourselves with brilliant thinkers, visionaries and hot-hearted disciples of Jesus by reading biographical accounts of great leaders from church history.

It is how we approach the reading of these works and what we learn from them that is important. Exciting, true events unfold within the covers of biographies. However, entertainment alone should not be our motivation for reading them. Neither should we look at these leaders as antiquated players in history, relevant only to their time and location. We need to evaluate their lives from various perspectives with the intention of learning practical lessons that will empower us to become world changers today. Here are some pointers gleaned over the years on how to benefit from biographies.

1. Maintain a perspective as to where the mentor fits in history.

Disassociating historical mentors from their place in history robs us of an important sense of perspective. Questions about the socio-political climate of a historical mentors' world need to be answered in order for us to meaningfully process the events of their life. It is usually helpful to construct a leadership time line and develop the historical setting out of which the time line arises. A leadership time line might include a series of phases such as foundations, inner life growth, ministry, and maturity. The length of each phase will vary and might span a decade or more. Such a time line would include important events in the individual's life as well as important historical events. This will allow you to evaluate the impact history had on the individual as well as the individual's impact on history.

For example, Samuel Mills' mother offered him to God for missionary service as a young boy. This is a noble act of faith in any generation. But when she did it, there were no North American mission agencies, and no one from this continent had gone out as a missionary! No wonder the idea stuck in young Samuel's mind. He eventually did play an important role in the formation of the first North American mission board along with the sending of America's first missionaries!

2. *Read with a sense of purpose—know what you are looking for.*

Identify the process items of each stage in the historical mentor's time line. Process items include the ways and means used by God to move a person along toward leadership. They may be events, people, circumstances, interventions, and inner life lessons. (If you would like to know more about the term, process item, read Robert Clinton's book, *The Making of a Leader.*) Look for clues to their leadership style, how they implement change, deal with failure or opposition. Make note of their methods. Were they innovators, reformers, or pioneers? Did they make extraordinary sacrifices or face difficult suffering?

3. *Become a member of the historical mentor's inner circle.*

Most great leaders get close to only a handful of people. The higher up the leadership ladder they climb, the more inaccessible they become to the broad base of their constituency. But through a biography, you can literally move into the inner circle of leaders who surrounded a historical mentor. You can sit in on board meetings, listen to private conversations, read personal letters and journal entries!

Just imagine you were given the opportunity to spend a week with James Dobson, Chuck Colson, Bill Bright, Loren Cunningham, or the leader of your choice. You could not ask questions; simply follow the leader and observe. At home, in the office, on the road, wherever they go. Would you do it? Of course you would! Future generations will probably get this opportunity by way of biographical writings. But you can access the inner circle of hundreds of great leaders not just for a week, but for the better part of a lifetime.

4. Identify the important windows of opportunity in the historical mentor's life.

In the developmental stages of most leaders, there are a few key windows of opportunity through which the primary focus of their ministry is opened. Much can be learned from identifying and evaluating those key moments. How did God prepare the mentors for these opportunities? How long did they prepare? Did they have a sense of destiny regarding their ministry focus? How rapidly did their ministry unfold after the windows of opportunity were opened? What were the key factors in their decision to take new steps of faith?

5. Identify the historical mentor's ultimate contribution.

The term, "ultimate contribution" comes from the studies of leadership emergence theory at Fuller Seminary of World Missions. An ultimate contribution is defined as a lasting legacy of Christian workers for which they are remembered and which furthers the cause of Christianity by one or more of the following: setting standards for life and ministry, impacting lives by enfolding them into God's Kingdom or developing them once in the Kingdom, serving as a stimulus for change, leaving behind an organization, institution or movement that serves as a channel through which God can work, or the discovery or promotion of ideas and communication that further God's work.

When evaluating the lives of historical mentors, there are scores of potential categories for ultimate contributions. A specific research project identified twelve primary categories for ultimate contributions or lasting legacies from the lives of missionaries. These twelve categories are listed in the chart below.

Ultimate Contribution/ Lasting Legacy	Thrust of Contribution
Saint	living a model life
Stylistic Practitioner	demonstrating a model ministry style
Mentor	productive ministry with individuals
Public Rhetorician	productive ministry with large groups
Crusader	rights wrongs and injustices in society
Artist	creative breakthroughs
Founder	starts new organizations
Stabilizer	solidifies organizations
Researcher	develops new ideation
Writer	captures new ideation for the use of others
Promoter	distributes effectively new ideation
Pioneer	founds apostolic type works

Keep in mind that there will likely be some overlap between these categories, and most leaders will make more than one ultimate contribution.

6. *Keep a quote on file that summarizes a main principle you have gleaned from the historical mentor.*

Many people have read biographies of great leaders but can remember very little, if anything, about them. One of the best ways to glean the most from historical mentors is by collecting quotes that summarize a key principle from their lives. If you do not actually memorize a quote, try to at least learn the details of an important vignette from the historical mentor's life.

It is helpful to write down a quote and share it with other people for several months as a means of reinforcing it. While you are learning the details of a vignette, share them with others for as long as it takes to lock those details into your memory.

Reading and Learning From Biographies is Biblical!

This book began with a threefold admonition from Hebrews 13:7. *Remember your leaders. Consider the outcome of their way of life. Imitate their faith.* Take advantage of the countless opportunities to "follow the leaders" through historical mentoring. As you do, keep in mind, it is not their lives we seek to imitate, but their faith.

About Kingdom Building Ministries

The mission of Kingdom Building Ministries (KBM) is to partner with the body of Christ to raise up new generations of laborers for Kingdom service worldwide.

CORE VALUES:

The Kingdom - More than just a future reality, the Kingdom for which we labor is the active, present rule of God among us.

Laborers - More than numerical church growth, laborers are the greatest need for worldwide harvest.

Prayer - Human effort is not enough, intercessory prayer is Jesus' strategy for raising up laborers.

Mentoring - True laborers cannot be mass produced, they are raised up through life on life mentoring.

Multiplication - Addition falls short, spiritual multiplication is the only way to raise laborers in sufficient numbers.

KBM is committed to preparing people to enter their field of ministry, whether it is as a full-time vocational worker, or as a layperson. Each of us has a calling and a purpose from God to fulfill in our lifetime. Our commitment to prepare you includes:

- **Itinerant Speakers.** KBM has men and women who desire to share with your church, retreat or campus how to live out Kingdom values in today's world.

- **Additional Resources.** There are many books and tape series available from KBM on kingdom issues. Designed to prepare individuals for service, topics include mentoring, missions and others.

- **The Laborer's Network (TLN).** *The Laborer's Network* couples laborers with a local mentor for twelve lessons and application exercises. The training is practical and equips the laborer to be a multiplier.

- **The Laborer's Institute (TLI).** *The Laborer's Institute* is our three month training school, allowing the laborer to develop deeper spiritual disciplines and receive training in various ministry avenues.

For more information on these and other opportunities available through Kingdom Building Ministries, call or write to us at:

Kingdom Building Ministries
14140 East Evans Avenue
Denver, CO 80014
E-mail: Laborers@kbm.org
Web Site: http://www.kbm.org
1-800-873-8957

Order Form

It's My Turn T-Shirts:
100% preshrunk cotton, natural color, colored logo on the front, *The Laborer's Declaration* on the back

It's My Turn Hats:
Two-toned, brushed canvas, semi-structured hat with colored logo on the front

It's My Turn Posters:
17" x 22" color poster of *The Laborer's Declaration*

T-Shirt and Hat designed by *Know Him*™
For other Know Him™ Christian Apparel call 1-888-2KNOWHIM

Item	Description	Price	Qty.	Total
1706	*It's My Turn* Book	$8.00		
1745	*It's My Turn* T-Shirt	$15.00		
1763	*It's My Turn* Hat	$15.00		
1764	*It's My Turn* Poster	$3.00		

Shipping: $3.00 or 10% of Subtotal

Subtotal: $ _____

Shipping: $ _____

Total: $ _____

Mail to: Kingdom Building Ministries
14140 E. Evans Avenue
Denver, CO 80014

Payment Method:
___ Check Enclosed ___ MasterCard
___ Discover ___ Visa

Ordered by:

Name _____

Address_____

_____

Phone _____

Exp. Date: _____

Card No.: _____

Signature: _____